My Walk to Clarity

How clarity, connection and self-care can change your life

MATT WALLACE

Copyright

Title: My Walk to Clarity: How clarity, connection and self-care can change your life

First published in October 2022

ISBN 9798849309194

This book is for anyone who's ever felt lonely or isolated.

Contents

Acknowledgements

My family and friends are the reason I am still alive to tell this story; I will always be grateful to them. I want to thank all my sponsors, funders, members, and everyone who has invested in Clarity Walk over the years. You have helped make this book possible.

Thank you for believing in me.

Scotland's leading dental group
clydemunrodental.com

Health and performance, naturally
niallrooney.co.uk

Your local recruitment experts
brookstreet.co.uk

Highlands based Ecological Consultants
a9consulting.co.uk

Foreword

Every now and then you meet someone who has a profound impact on you, not because of their wealth or flamboyance, but because of their genuineness and passion. Matt Wallace, Founder of Clarity Walk, has such a strong desire to help others avoid treading the path he did you can taste it!

I make no apologies for pushing Matt to write this book; he has a story that must be shared.

Matt has been to the gates of hell, and through a twist of fate those gates remained closed. His life's work is to ensure that the gate remains firmly closed for you too.

This book is Matt's journey, Matt's story. What makes it really scary? It could just as easily be mine or yours...

I am proud to call Matt a friend, and now he's your friend too.

Stuart Mason

(Director of Here's How To)

Introduction

"There is no Wi-Fi in the forest, but I promise you will find a better connection."

Ralph Smart

Hi. I'm Matt. This is the story of how I overcame suicidal depression and founded a social enterprise, Clarity Walk, to support people's mental health and wellbeing.

I will share everything from how I spiralled down to the point of suicide to how I climbed out of the darkness. I will provide you with the exact methods that helped me take back control of my life.

This book is a work of non-fiction based on my life, experiences, and recollections. Certain details in this story, including names (where appropriate), have been changed to protect identity and privacy. It's possible that other people may have very different perspectives and recollections of shared events; I've shared from my heart and from my own take on those past events.

If what I've shared can help just one person, ideally you, take charge of their mental wellbeing then I have done my job.

Why I wrote this book

This is my first book. I have never dreamed of becoming an author but have always had a passion to help others. Surviving the darkness and overcoming many life challenges made me realise my story had to be shared.

It is for anyone who has ever felt isolated, alone or overwhelmed. It can support you or someone you know.

What this book covers

This book covers a variety of relatable topics, including depression, suicide, toxic relationships, and stress.

How to use this book

The book is conversational and designed to make you think throughout. It is filled with actionable advice to help you make decisions in your own life.

Resources

At the end of the book, I've listed resources that might help you.

Please note: There are sections of this book that may not be appropriate reading for anyone under the age of 16.

Chapter 1

The early years

"Vulnerability sounds like truth and feels like courage. Truth and courage aren't always comfortable, but they're never weakness."

Brené Brown

I didn't have the best childhood and not for the reasons most origin stories start.

There was no poverty, abusive parents, poor education or one 'significant traumatic event' that had the power to 'change everything.'

I was born in Inverness (Highlands of Scotland), a beautiful city rich in scenery and filled with captivating forests and greenspaces to explore and connect. My friends and I spent most of our time playing outdoors and going on adventures. I am glad we had the opportunity; there was no social media, no reliance on online games, or any other major distractions that could rob us of this experience.

My family wasn't rich or poor. We didn't have designer clothes or extravagant presents, but we were not struggling for basic necessities. I had friends who were given everything; I felt jealous. I thought it was unfair that my parents didn't value me enough to give me more; I had to do chores to earn anything that was given to me.

However, my parents knew they were teaching me the value of hard work. They knew it would motivate me and help build life skills that I could use in the future. Many of my friends grew up without any drive or ambition because they expected success to just come to them. I am thankful that my parents taught me these lessons; it has made me the person I am today.

What was different about me was my appearance. I was gaunt, had acne, and a large nose. By society's standards I felt ugly. This led to children who were not my friends relentlessly bullying me using anything and everything as a verbal weapon. It started off with a small number of people in the latter years of primary school; it got significantly worse when I was in High School as there were more people to see my vulnerabilities and take aim.

They might have seen it as just a joke or just having a laugh, but to me it was so much more. It didn't stop.

Going to school knowing I was going to be turned into a joke and put down each day was agonising. Sometimes

I would laugh along with the jokes and pretend everything was ok; I hoped that would help me fit in, but even with a smile on my face I was dying inside. I just wanted to belong but I felt like an outcast.

Each attempt to try and fit in was shot down and my confidence was shattered. I walked around with my head in my chest and feared making eye contact with others. I didn't want to receive more put downs.

I used to be happy without a care in the world. My experience with school changed that. I saw most people as a threat and I just expected the worst. There were times I wasn't nice either as I was holding onto so much pain and frustration.

Some of these children even started a rumour that I had sex with my dog as well as many other things that added to the torment. The abuse directed towards me was never physical, but in some ways, I wish it was; it would have been easier to deal with a punch or kick than a barrage of negative comments each day. It wrecked my self-esteem and left me with trauma that would haunt me through the years (and tear down my self-worth.)

I used to ask myself:

> *"What have I done to deserve this? Will this continue for the rest of my life?"*

I constantly asked myself these questions. I felt completely worthless and unloved by society which led me to a very dark place and left me depressed. To avoid the pain of dealing with these bullies I started to skip school and pretend to be ill so I could stay at home. Home was my safe place free from the words of hate.

No matter how many days I spent at home the bullying left its impact. I would frequently fantasise about not being alive anymore. I wondered what it would be like to not have to deal with what my life had become. I didn't share my thoughts with friends or family as I didn't want to be a burden. This pain was mine. I managed to keep it a secret, fake happiness, and pretend that everything was fine.

As time went on the darkness started to consume me without so much as a glimmer of light. It felt like the only answer was to end the pain (and my horrible existence.)

I needed to take my own life. I felt it had to be done; I had a plan.

My attempt to end the suffering

One day I called in sick to school, a day that I knew my parents would not be at home. I took what I thought would be my last walk downstairs to the medicine cupboard, gathered up every pill I could find and took them back to my room.

My room was small, dimly lit and scarred from where the wallpaper had been stripped. It looked run down.

I didn't feel sad or happy. I experienced an unusual sense of numbness. I was simply providing a solution to the problems of a 14-year-old boy, and I couldn't see any other way.

I crawled back into bed and made myself comfy with the pills resting on top of the bedcovers. I cracked them out of their packs and placed all 30 of them in my hands. I smirked, confident that it was all going to be over soon. Then I did it. One by one I swallowed the pills until there was nothing left but empty packets and a quiet room. I shut my eyes to go to sleep for what I thought would be the final time. I was ready for the pain to be over.

Or so I thought.

After 30 minutes I woke up with excruciating shooting pains in my stomach that forced me to rush to the toilet and brought me to my knees. I was vomiting intensely and threw up every single pill. My plan had failed.

My only thought was that I was so pathetic I couldn't even kill myself. Surely it was simple. I was still depressed, but I was no longer motivated to kill myself as I didn't want to risk failing again.

I decided to run away to the forest and thought that perhaps I'd let 'the elements' take me instead. I wrote a note for my parents, packed clothes, water, food and a sleeping bag, and got on my bike. I only reached the bottom of the street when I decided I couldn't go any further. I was temporarily frozen in time; deep down I had already realised this was more of a knee-jerk reaction than a well thought out plan. I cycled back to the house and ran a hot bath so that I could 'steam in my thoughts' and get clear on what I wanted.

I forgot about one thing though; the note to my parents was still on the sideboard. How could I have forgotten about that? Later that day my mum saw the note; I think at first she was confused, perhaps thinking it was some kind of sick joke. The reality and enormity of that note was difficult for her; until that point, I hadn't given any thought to the impact on the people around me. Needless to say, when she read it she was absolutely broken, beyond devastated, (or more accurately, she was heartbroken after she read it 20 times and the reality of what I had written had really sunk in.)

She came to me to have a heartfelt conversation; we talked for hours about what I needed, and what we could do together. That was the first time I had ever opened up about my feelings in this way. The pain was starting to ease because I shared it. We both knew it would come back though, so we agreed that help was needed. The first step was both of us going to see a GP; I was referred to therapy. The journey out of the darkness was beginning...

In the therapy chair

I was incredibly nervous for the first therapy session, but the psychologist helped me feel at ease and allowed me to talk without any judgement. It was nice to talk openly and honestly. I had bottled up how others were treating me for years.

Therapy helped me unload my thoughts and feelings whilst teaching me valuable skills to build my confidence. I no longer felt as vulnerable; I no longer walked with my head down to my chest. I started to learn how to connect with others and defend myself when needed. Over time the bullying lessened to a degree that I could live with. I managed to finish school with good qualifications, but still no clear plan of what I wanted to do (until that point so much of my school life had been about survival.)

I highly recommend therapy; it is not weak to ask for support, and it can help give you your life back. I wish I had continued to go to therapy to help me overcome issues that arose later in life.

My school years were some of the hardest I have ever experienced. The trauma from bullying haunted me. I could still hear the words 'you are useless', 'you shouldn't be here', 'you will never amount to anything' ringing in my ears. They were hard to ignore, especially when I was experiencing difficult times because they became louder than ever. Developing a healthy routine and having people to speak to has always helped me.

Looking back, I wish I had told someone what I was experiencing and asked for help sooner. I would rather have been called a snitch than feel I needed to take my own life. I wish I had been assertive and told my bullies that what they were saying was not okay; many aren't even aware that they are bullying someone and might have stopped if they had seen its impact. I wish I had done a lot of things differently when it came to bullying, but I hope my experiences can provide lessons for others.

How bullying has evolved

I am thankful that I grew up in a time without social media as my home remained a safe place. Today there are even more pressures for children and youth to be perfect. Constant comparison clearly divides the haves and the have nots, which can lead to an increase in bullying.

It's now often 24/7 as there are multiple ways to create torment through social media, photoshopping and direct messaging. These posts and messages are not fleeting like a verbal word; they are around for hours, days or months until deleted (and even then if someone has taken a screenshot it might start all over again.) Home is no longer a safe place; I feel for the children of today.

That said, bullying doesn't just affect children. It impacts anyone regardless of their age, gender, looks, background, or profession. It can create trauma and deeply impact on mental health. Although there are many theories around why someone becomes a bully, I think it's time to accept that for one reason or another, some people are simply 'horrible.'

In search of a lucky break

Having experienced more than my fair share of 'horrible' people, I was looking for a release from the emotional pain.

I had no career direction and ended up working in a variety of minimum wage jobs, including retail and hospitality. For a brief period of time, I was even one of those annoying canvassers that chap on your front door trying to sell you stuff.

I was coasting.

I worked in a hotel for a few years exchanging long hard hours for pennies. I always wished I earned more so I could reap the benefits of my hard work. You have to be careful what you wish for though; my friends introduced me to the world of online gambling. It was exciting, flashy, new and there were promises that I could soon be making thousands of pounds. My friends told me how much money they were making, and that I could easily do the same. On minimum wage this was obviously a very attractive proposition, so I decided to go for it and play my first game of online poker.

I created an account and deposited £50.

My friends taught me the basics of how it worked, including how to tell if someone is bluffing, when to raise, and most importantly, how to win. I learnt about tournaments, cash games and more. The idea of making more money with less effort excited me.

Time to up the stakes; I felt ready to win so I entered a small 10-man poker tournament. Applying all the rules my friends taught me I could see that it was working as I was winning hands, calling bluffs, and increasing my chip stack. With each hand I got a shot of dopamine from the risk versus reward, it was thrilling to see how each game would play out. By the end of the game, I was in the top three and managed to double the money I'd put in. It was exhilarating, addictive, and I saw an opportunity to quickly earn a lot more money. I played a few games that day and made a small £40 profit, but the stakes would get much higher.

It wasn't long before I started investing more. I loved the thrill. I would win games and I would lose, but I came out on top most of the time. I was easily making £50+ per day, which soon increased to up to £150 per day (occasionally more.) As someone who was working in a minimum wage job I was addicted to how easy it was to gamble and make money.

I would wake up and go to bed thinking about it. I was obsessed. It was so much fun, until it wasn't. When I was winning I felt in control and on top of the world, and even when I was losing I felt in control as it was my money and I was making all the decisions. Poker was my way of controlling something in a life where I mostly felt powerless.

There was a game when I decided to up the ante and play for £500+ one on one. The thrill of playing for this kind of money was unlike any other. We made minimal investment and tested each other's skill (or luck) with a few hands. My opponent would win a hand, then I would win a hand. This went on for a while until I would get a hand that would change everything; a pair of aces.

This is the best hand you could start with, and in a one-on-one setting it can be a very smart move to raise high or go all in preflop (before cards are revealed), so that is exactly what I did. The other player bided his time trying to decide if he would call or not. I was praying that he would. The clock ticked down, and in the final seconds he called with a pair of 3s (a lower hand compared to my aces.)

I thought it was so stupid for him to call so I did a small dance and smiled believing I would be £500 up, but that smile didn't last long. The last card placed on the virtual table was not in my favour. It was another three; he won with three of a kind. I lost everything.

As I stared at the computer screen I couldn't believe that I had lost so much money in a short space of time. Rage consumed me. In anger, I smashed a plate against the wall.

> *'This shouldn't have happened! I had a pair of aces, but I'll win it back. It was just a bad beat.'*

Luck was not on my side that night. Instead of stopping I deposited more money and started to play to try to re-coup my £500. I was sure I had the skills and the knowledge to do so.

However, in a mist of red I started playing recklessly and lost more and more money. I was playing from an emotional place, and without any logic. I deposited more, then lost more; I didn't care. All I saw were numbers on a screen with nothing tangible in my hand. I did this all night until the last deposit read:

> *'You have insufficient funds in your account to make a deposit.'*

I logged into my bank account and it took a moment for me to register that all I had left was £5.67. All the money I had made playing poker was gone! Everything I had earned from the hotel was gone. I was stressed, empty and confused. They say the house always wins.

I went back to work feeling deflated knowing that all my previous work had been for nothing, but I couldn't stop thinking about poker and how I'd just had a 'bad night.' I convinced myself that I could get back on top, so I did something that was extremely stupid. I took out a large bank loan so that I could play more poker.

I would win a few games, and lose even more. The £2,500 bank loan was quick to dwindle and the thought of paying it back ate my soul. All my mind thought about was playing more poker and how I would get it all back and be on top again, but the balance plummeted to zero and I entered a high state of anxiety. How would I pay back the £2,500? With my mind ripped apart from the financial pressure I plucked up the courage to ask my parents to lend me the £2,500. Thankfully they did. It was safer for me to owe them than owe the bank which might negatively impact my future in some way.

> *'Do you think I learnt my lesson? No, I lied to myself and promised not to do it again, but I knew I was obsessed with the game of cards.'*

This led to me gambling in secret. I even took out another large loan to feed my addiction. It wasn't just me though, I found out that my friends also lost money, and like any gambler they would only share the wins not the losses. Over the year I lost £7,000, which was just under three-quarters of what I could earn in a year working at the hotel.

I became extremely stressed, depressed, and had suicidal thoughts again. It felt as though I was only living to pay off debt. I even started buying lottery tickets and literally praying for a win to solve my issues. These prayers were never answered; I had to deal with it myself. The years of 18-20 were simply taken from me. There were no nights out, no holidays, no cars, just an ugly pile of debt to pay off that was entirely of my own making.

I knew I had a problem. I knew I needed to stop. This was killing me. I had no money left to gamble with, so I started to look at ways that I could break free and reclaim my life. I wanted to go cold turkey; trying to do things in moderation never works for me. If I am drawn to a tiny taste of anything I end up in a buffet of overindulgence. I could no longer afford to lose. To help me break free I excluded myself from the regular sites I used so that I could no longer play. However, sometimes I would re-lapse after seeing an advert and fantasising about money. Occasionally I'd find a new site and get my fix, while also losing £50 or £100 in the process.

Over the years I managed to take control of my gambling habit and pay back the bank and my parents. I was debt free! It was a huge relief as I could now work to live rather than simply live to pay off debt.

I also realised how susceptible I was to a fully blown gambling habit. The accountability lay with me; my choices and my actions were up to me. Addiction means you're always in recovery; you are not suddenly fixed. You must set rules and boundaries to protect yourself from relapse.

Greed is a powerful force that can manipulate and twist your character and decisions. You might spiral into sports betting or playing slot machines, poker, roulette or other forms of gambling. The risk versus reward of every game provides an intoxicating thrill, and entices you to up the stakes and do it more frequently. It is not something to be taken lightly.

Gambling can ruin lives, destroy families, and lead to other compulsions such as alcohol and drugs. If you haven't started, don't. If you are already gambling I've provided a useful resource in the appendices.

A weight lifted

Becoming debt-free allowed me to do so much more with my life; I was able to socialise with my friends, go to the cinema, enjoy meals and nights out. However, these nights would often negatively impact my mindset as they frequently conjured up feelings of the past. I was physically fit and active but I was also so skinny that I was barely able to fill out a t-shirt. I felt unattractive; the nights out proved that to me because my friends would get attention from women whilst I was simply ignored (or came across as weird when trying to speak to people.)

I felt anxious around groups of people. I compared myself to them and constantly worried about being judged, all of which made it difficult to relax. I slowly stopped going on nights out as it would lead to me feeling low and unwanted; alcohol exposed how I truly felt about myself. I didn't want to slip back into a depression so I found other ways to socialise with my friends.

Then it all changed.

My friends introduced me to the gym and the world of weightlifting. I'd been in gyms before and used the weight machines and did cardio exercise, but I didn't know what the hell I was doing so I didn't make much progress.

The gym my friends went to was like no other; it had huge open spaces filled with high tech equipment, weights and lots of beautiful bodies. I was mesmerised by it, ready to learn and desperate to get involved!

We warmed up with a variety of exercises and stretches then went onto the bench press which is a staple exercise for raw strength to build your arms, chest, and shoulders. I was shown the correct technique, the tempo of the lift, and how I should breathe whilst doing it.

I felt ready and with instruction I slid under the bar, gripped it tightly, and took it off the rack. As I lowered it to my chest I felt my muscles stretch and expand before pushing the bar forcefully to the ceiling. Repeat. During each rep I could feel my muscles become tighter and tighter. I did twelve reps altogether and felt completely pumped; my muscles were pulsating, my eyes wide and testosterone took over! This new sensation was incredible, and even with those few reps I felt stronger, more confident, and I could feel my body coming back to life. I knew that I wanted more, and I couldn't wait to get back in the gym.

I discovered the best exercises to build muscle and strength; this included the deadlift, bench press, squat, shoulder press, rows and much more to help me build a great routine. I went to the gym three to four times per week and I also researched the best foods to eat to build muscle which included high protein foods, drinking protein shakes, getting enough calories, drinking plenty of water, and making sure that I was getting plenty of rest between workouts.

It wasn't long before I could see results. I started to bulk up and build strength, both of which helped me feel confident. I rebuilt my body and my mind. As well as going to the gym I started using sunbeds and dressing more 'fashionably.' A few months in and my body changed completely. I was no longer skinny; I packed on enough muscle to finally fill a t-shirt! I felt physically attractive, something I had never experienced before.

This opened the door to a new level of confidence which made me feel like I could do anything! I felt happy enough to join my friends on nights out (without the debilitating anxiety.) I no longer felt judged and was able to chat to anyone, including women! For the first time in my life, I felt that I was in control and fitted in. It was my way of showing my bullies that I was worthy and successful.

Each week I'd go to the gym, go to work, and on nights out so that I could socialise, dance and meet new people. On the inevitable hangover Sunday, I would devour my cheat meal, a 20" Domino's pizza with cheese, chicken, sweetcorn, and pineapple (pineapple is delicious on a pizza, and I won't be told otherwise!.) The pizza was routinely followed by a whole tub of Ben and Jerry's Cookie Dough ice cream; I'd inhale the whole thing!

Life felt good; my confidence skyrocketed. However, this confidence turned to arrogance, and I started to hang around the wrong people to be one of the 'lads' and be a 'player' thanks to my newfound ability to attract women. I enjoyed the attention and felt that fitness had taken me from nothing to something.

Pay it forward

I wanted to share my enthusiasm for fitness; especially with people who felt bad about themselves or lacked confidence.

I enrolled with the University of the Highlands and Islands to gain an HND in Fitness, Health and Exercise so that I could become a personal trainer(PT). I was surrounded by students who were in great shape and passionate about using fitness as a tool for transformation. The energy was electric; we supported each other through the first year's assignments and tests. I learnt an abundance of skills that set me in good stead for my career as a PT.

However, during the first year I was still hanging out with all the wrong people at weekends and this had serious repercussions.

One evening my friend and I were at a nightclub. The DJs were pumping out the latest dance music. We had the VIP area to ourselves complete with a luxury couch and a bottle of vodka; we wanted to feel like kings!

As we stepped down from the VIP area my friend was threatened by a man and his brother; there'd previously been some bad blood between them. I don't like violence or conflict, plus I was nursing a leg injury so I pulled my friend away and we went for a walk to try to de-escalate the situation.

Fifteen minutes later we returned to the VIP area. The man from before was lounging on our couch as though it was his throne. I felt angry. I asked him to get off the couch and leave. He stared at me so I repeated the request telling him we just wanted to have a peaceful night out. He tried to punch me but I managed to dodge it. A red mist consumed me and with my good leg I sprung up into the air and provided justice from above by delivering an explosive punch that dazed him to the couch.

He got to his feet and took a second swing at me. I put him in a headlock and smeared his face across the wall before tossing him towards the bouncers to deal with. I was angry because I'd become caught up in the conflict. In an attempt to recover a good night out I drank a lot. I became extremely intoxicated and unaware of my surroundings after downing approximately 15 Jägerbombs (and multiple vodka and cokes.)

Somewhere in the distance I became aware of yelling; I realised that the brother of the man who'd been throwing punches earlier was approaching us. I didn't want more violence but in my drunken state I was slow to react.

Boom! A thunderous punch rocked me backwards causing my mouth to bleed heavily. The bouncers were quick to restrain the man, but because I'd been involved in both incidents I was asked to leave the club.

As I staggered towards the hotel where I worked I realised my lip was bust open and my face was very messed up. One of my colleagues called a taxi to take me to Accident and Emergency to have my lip stitched. It was so swollen and painful I could barely open my mouth.

Even though I was still drunk I was questioning why this had happened, and whether or not I deserved it. I hated violence. I just wanted a drama-free night out!

The following morning, I realised I wasn't going to be able to eat any solid foods because my mouth hurt so much. I asked my mum to bring me a syringe (minus the needle!), so I could feed myself liquids. For the next week I was on a liquid diet.

My mum was shocked to see the sorry state that I was in. She couldn't believe someone could do this to her boy. We drove to the police station where I gave a statement. I was so angry at what had happened, but my voice was muffled and unintelligible because I couldn't open my mouth properly!

I took sick leave for a couple of weeks; a bashed-up face doesn't go well with hospitality! I lost a lot of weight; all of this negatively impacted my mind. I took the time to reflect and realised that it was likely none of the drama would have happened if I'd been socialising with different people. I dug a bit deeper and unearthed the realisation that I was hanging out with the 'wrong crowd' because I wanted to be cool. The truth is they weren't 'my people' and I was putting on a facade to try to fit in. I didn't even like the character I was portraying; I was usually a friendly, chilled out person who enjoys the gym, Star Wars, and video games!

I didn't enjoy pretending to be someone else or any of the conflict (including inner conflict) that came with it. I decided to drop the facade, cut the ties with the crowd that wasn't a good fit, and be me again.

A month later my face had healed; I was back in the gym and quickly regained my shape and strength. I felt happy. However, the trauma of the assault made me anxious about future nights out; I couldn't afford to be injured like that again.

I returned to my studies edging closer to my exciting goal of becoming a personal trainer. I didn't hold back on being my true self. I did more of what I really enjoyed instead of regretting drunken nights out.

When one becomes two

As I mentioned earlier, I'd been enjoying the novelty of being popular with women, but apart from the odd hook-up or quick fling I had no meaningful relationships. I was happy in my own little bubble doing things that I enjoyed and working on myself. I didn't want to let anyone else interfere with that, until one night...

For the first time in a long time, I decided to go out with some friends. We'd opted for quieter venues because I wanted to avoid being attacked. Even though I was unable to fully relax I still had fun and felt confident enough to chat to the people around me.

In one of the bars a beautiful woman caught my attention. For ease, let's call her Hayley (not her real name.)

Hayley's eyes were like emeralds. Her dazzling smile could light up a room. Without any fear or hesitation, I walked over to Hayley, introduced myself, and invited her to join me for a drink. She agreed!

We found a quiet spot in the bar to enjoy a drink together. Over a vodka and coke and a gin and tonic (her choice), we hit it off. Hayley had a fun, bubbly personality that made me smile. She was intelligent and we had fantastic in-depth conversations about all sorts. One drink turned into several; we chatted and danced until the bars closed. I had no doubt that Hayley was special.

We met up many times and it wasn't long until we were in a relationship; this was a big deal for me as it was the first person I'd let in since I managed to turn my life around, but it felt right. Finally, I felt ready for a serious relationship.

The first few months were great; Hayley and I enjoyed adventures in nature, cinema dates and made the most of each other's company. It wasn't long before we were openly saying I love you to each other and lived happily ever after.

It sounds romantic doesn't it? However, if it sounds too good to be true that's because it was!

My friends and family would often comment that Hayley wasn't right for me. I ignored them. I was blinded by love. She was special to me, and I wanted the relationship to be the right fit!

Even now people tell me that I should have just left the relationship, but perhaps you know that it's not always that easy. When you've already experienced trauma there's often a lingering lack of self-worth. You're easily broken by people who see themselves as better than you. Even when I began to realise that Hayley and I weren't right together, I didn't want to face the emptiness I expected to feel without her in my life.

I wanted to see Hayley as perfect; I made myself oblivious to anything that wasn't perfect. If I did raise any issues I felt that she distracted me with sex, after which I'd promptly forget about the problem!

Others could see me slowly get broken down to the point I would barely see friends. Hayley became my life.

I wasn't aware how different my life had become, but often when you are being coercively controlled (as I felt I was) everything is so subtle and gradual that you aren't aware at the time. Hayley used small phrases and actions which would influence my decisions, undermine me, and decrease my self-esteem. I was like a dog on a lead delighted to follow its owner's commands. She knew my weaknesses and I felt she would use them to control me by commenting on my looks, career prospects, and the fact that I was a student with no money.

There were two situations that I still remember vividly.

1. The first was a discussion around how I couldn't afford to go on holiday. Hayley told me that if we didn't go on holiday together we might as well break up.

She paid for us both to go on holiday and I borrowed spending money from my parents. Even though I had agreed to go, I felt controlled, and pathetic.

2. The second situation I remember was a conversation about how excited I was to become a personal trainer. Hayley told me I would not make it as a PT. She couldn't see why someone would pay to exercise when they could go and do it for free. She followed this up by telling me that they certainly wouldn't pay for me.

I felt like Hayley undermined my goals and my career plans. I thought perhaps she realised that if my career took off she'd lose some control over me. There were multiple phrases and moments like this peppered throughout our relationship; some were subtle and some were major red flags!

One evening we both went to a rave at a nightclub with some of my friends. It was full of lasers and strobe lights, and pumping music that put my energy through the roof. My friends and I were in our element and kept hitting the dance floor but when we returned I realised that Hayley had been chatting to the same guy for a long time. I discovered that it was her ex-boyfriend. Alarm bells were ringing loud and clear. I was furious; we ditched her for the night and moved onto another club.

The next day Hayley came to my house. I was suspicious because I sensed that something was going on with her ex. Hayley promised it was nothing.

However, my guts told me otherwise so when she left the room I did something I've never done before; I read her text messages. There was a mountain of messages between Hayley and her ex. They were discussing sex, meeting up again, and how much they missed each other.

I was uncontrollably angry. I erupted and yelled at Hayley to leave and never come back. She looked sheepish as she drove away. I think she was surprised that I had the capacity to intimidate her.

I was suddenly single. I vented about the poor relationship to my friends and family only to hear them say:

> *"We told you. We tried to help."*

It was time to get on with my life. Four weeks later I needed a distraction so went on a night out with a couple of women I knew fairly well (or at least I thought I did.)

Adding insult to injury

You know what young, heartbroken men do, don't you? They get straight back on the horse.

I went to the home of these two female friends, and we started off drinking vodka, shots, and anything else I could get my hands on to numb the pain of betrayal. By the time we headed into town (the big city of Inverness) I was drunk. We continued to drink and dance; at some point I must have blacked out.

The next thing I remember is walking towards an ambulance with my friend and a bartender. I wondered what the hell was going on.

> *"What happened to me?".*
>
> *"You've been attacked and you need to go to hospital", the bartender told me.*

I put my hand over my eye and could feel the blood pouring from it.

As I got into the ambulance I found out that I'd been attacked by a group of Polish men (one of the women I was with was Polish.) I didn't understand why it had happened, but I was angry and upset; two assaults within a year! Why did people keep sucker punching me? The word 'why' played on repeat in my mind.

At A&E two large cuts above my eye and one below my cheek were stitched. I was concussed. I was questioned by the police even though my mumblings likely made minimal sense.

It turned out that the girl I was dancing with used to date

one of the Polish guys. She was winding him up to show that she was over him. This made me feel even more upset and angry; I don’t like to be a pawn in anyone’s game!

Broken, bruised, and scarred I felt vulnerable again and became particularly wary of Polish men. Even though I would still act friendly, have good conversations and share laughs with them, I couldn't shake off the feeling that I might be in danger. Common sense and life experience tells me that one person doesn't represent an entire country, but my trauma lived on.

I was concussed for a full month. I frequently forgot what I was doing. I forgot people’s names. I failed my first driving test because I tried to do a hill start in neutral. The assault also affected my speech. I developed a stutter and mixed up my words which often left me feeling embarrassed and lacking confidence.

As you can imagine I was vulnerable, vulnerable enough that when I received a phone call from ‘the ex’, Hayley. I agreed to meet her. She had heard about the assault and wanted to comfort me. I was hooked; our toxic relationship was back.

Even though I experienced all this I still managed to finish the first year of my HND in Inverness in 2012. I was on track and one step closer to becoming a personal trainer. I needed to complete my second year of studies in Glasgow, which meant I would be in a long-distance relationship.

Needless to say, Hayley wasn't happy; perhaps because she'd have less control over me! It was exciting to live in a new place and enjoy new experiences. I made the leap.

Glasgow itself is a magnificent city buzzing with life, culture and so many things to do compared to Inverness. I found the atmosphere of the city friendlier and more welcoming than the Highlands. I knew this city was right for me.

The hotel I worked at helped me transfer to a new hotel so I still had my own income, and I found a city centre flatshare with a guy we'll call Craig (more on that shortly) that was only a 20 minute train journey to the college in Anniesland.

The lecturers were knowledgeable, supportive, encouraging, and very friendly providing me with multiple opportunities that would benefit my career. My peers were also supportive; we had great camaraderie.

Continuous growth

The second year of my Fitness, Health and Exercise course was completely different. It included practical elements that built upon the theory elements of the first year.

I learnt how to:

- Understand the needs of new clients by completing wellness questionnaires
- Assess the current ability of a client

- Create a bespoke exercise programme
- Teach spin or cycle classes
- Teach exercise to music (aerobics, step, bums and tums!)

The knowledge I gained was invaluable. I was hungry to learn. The lecturers recognised my drive and offered me a position in the college gym where I could help the other students and run a weekly cycle session for the lecturers. I gladly accepted knowing that it would be valuable for my CV.

I saw Hayley every three weeks; we would text, call or video call every day. We broke up again during that time as I wanted to feel free, but my own insecurities meant we always got back together. However, my new life meant that 'her hold' over me was weakening.

A snake in the grass

My flatmate Craig (not his real name), who had seemed okay at first (a bit of a nerd like me so I thought we'd get on), started to take control of our living space. He set up his gaming computer in the living room and spent countless hours playing games in a barely tied bathrobe (you get what I'm saying!) During these sessions Craig incessantly scratched his scruffy red beard and screamed at the screen trying to offend other players.

Needless to say, it was a bit much!

His mastery of the shared spaces was limited; the kitchen had oil splashed all over the worktops, there were scraps of food on the ground and a steady pile of unwashed dishes. Craig's mess attracted maggots. You might not want to know this, but this guy worked as a chef!

Empty cans of juice and chocolate wrappers littered the living room along with discarded clothes. I tried to get Craig to tidy up but it was a waste of effort. It got worse.

I was ironing my work clothes one day and as I looked at the drying rack, I saw one of my t-shirts on it. I knew I hadn't put it there.

I had noticed some of my clothes going missing for a while but, hands up, my room wasn't immaculate, so I'd put it down to that. The t-shirt got me curious.

When Craig went out I went into his room to investigate (I promise I am not in the habit of reading people's texts or poking about in their private spaces!) I was shocked to find my clothes scattered all around his bombsite of a bedroom! I could see my t-shirts and a pyramid stack of my underwear (one pair even had a skid mark on it!) This guy had been wearing my underwear; who even does that? I knew I had to move out.

I found a new flat, emailed the landlord and got my deposit back.

Moving into the new flat was a knee-jerk reaction, which

is a bit of a trait of mine that has often led to poor outcomes (and the occasional great one.) My new flat wasn't much better; there were no 'underwear thieves', but there were mice. I could hear them scratching inside the walls. They chewed my laptop and phone cables. It wasn't the best, but then, they didn't wear my underwear or leave skid marks so...

A dangerous encounter

While living in Glasgow the legal proceedings for the first assault got underway (the one from the night my friend and I were supposedly kings on our thrones.) I started to receive very serious threats.

The man who assaulted me was from a dangerous family; they had a network in Glasgow (why me?)

The threats were covert and came to me via other people, which meant they could easily be denied. The police told me they could 'do nothing', so I had to watch my back 24/7. I genuinely feared for my life (again.)

Unsurprisingly, my anxiety returned. Even though the mice weren't great company I barely left the flat. I felt distracted from my studies.

I could feel the fear setting in so deep that I made indirect contact with the family to say that I would drop the charges on the basis that I was drunk and could easily have been confused about the events of that night. I knew fine well what had happened, but I wasn't willing to spend the rest of my life looking over my shoulder. It was a weight off my mind which allowed me to get stuck into my college work.

This rollercoaster of a year went by in a flash. I became fully qualified with an HND in Fitness, Health and Exercise ready to be a personal trainer and help people transform mind and body. Even though I had some negative experiences in Glasgow (did I mention skid marks and mice!) I loved the city and wanted to make it my home. I started looking for career opportunities.

Sadly, this came to an abrupt halt because Hayley convinced me to move home. She refused to put up with a long-distance relationship any longer. Like a lapdog I packed up my belongings and trotted back to Inverness.

When I moved back to the Highlands, Hayley sensed that she had less control over me. Fortunately, which sounds bizarre, her behaviour had become more erratic and her attempts to keep me in line were more blatant. Everything became clear; if this woman stayed in my life I would never feel equal to her. I knew she would always try to control me and hamper my career.

My parents told me that if I stayed in the relationship with Hayley she would never be welcome in their house (my family home.) That sounds harsh, but I knew it was for my own good and that they wanted me to wake up and realise the negative influence she was having on me. I am thankful for the lesson.

After several weeks I summoned the strength to end the relationship. I met Hayley in person, looked her dead in the eye, told her that it was over, and walked away. Although it was the obvious solution (and you might even have been screaming at me to do it as you read the earlier tales), it was one of the hardest things I have ever done. It's hard to explain the hold that someone has over you, or the feelings that accompany these toxic dynamics.

I suddenly felt like I'd been unshackled; I was free to be my own person and take on the world. There were several attempts to lure me back into the relationship, but I was strong enough to resist.

At this point I knew that my career as a personal trainer was within my grasp. I was excited for the next chapter of my life which, surely without the presence of the 'wrong people', could only be magnificent (an assumption that turned out to be false!)

Chapter 2

The dark spiral

"Not until we are lost do we begin to understand ourselves."

Henry David Thoreau

My PT career began in 2014. I worked in a local gym in Inverness and had a part-time job to support me until I built up a larger client base. Like most 'fresh out of college' personal trainers, I thought people would flock to me eager to transform their lives. I soon realised this wasn't the case and it was going to be much harder than I thought! The beginning was a slow burn.

Inverness has a small population (and a predominantly elderly one at that) which was saturated with other well-established PTs.

However, out of sheer luck I managed to get a couple of clients to start building my experience and use what I learned in college to make a real impact. I was passionate and dedicated to providing excellent service and getting results. I dedicated many hours to check-ins, programming, nutrition support and creating content.

Applying what I had learnt in college to the real world was a steep learning curve; there were so many factors to consider with the main one being client adherence. I could create the best programme in the world but unless people followed through it was pointless. I had to find the balance of getting great results and what my clients would find enjoyable. I made mistakes and learnt the lessons required to build on my skills and experience.

Although I was improving as a personal trainer my business knowledge was non-existent. It became clear that the PT's who were the busiest were often the best marketers, not necessarily the best personal trainers!

With that in mind I studied and invested in a variety of marketing and business courses so that I could turn my passion into profit. After a lot of trial and error I started to stand out in a sea of personal trainers which led to more enquiries and bookings. I was beginning to see my dream of being a full-time PT come to life; within 18 months I was fully booked and quit my part-time job. I had money in the bank and felt proud that I had demonstrated that I was worth something after all! I had shown the bullies (even if they weren't paying any attention whatsoever!) that I wasn't useless!

To make the most of my knowledge I created online training and small group sessions so that I could provide more in a shorter space of time. This was the biggest earner for me and things were ticking along nicely. My internal dialogue changed from:

'Why me?'

to

'You made it, Matt! You finally made it!'

I was living the dream of helping my clients achieve their fitness goals and transform their lives.

I enjoyed many success stories including clients who:

- Overcame their injuries
- Trained for events
- Achieved a new level of fitness (even at an older age)
- Achieved the 'muscle tone' they wanted

I loved the impact I was having on the world.

I loved being my own boss.

The lonely entrepreneur

The personal training lifestyle sounds great doesn't it? However, most people won't tell you how lonely it feels to be a business owner. You will invest countless hours working at antisocial times with your mind fixated on how you can improve, get better results or make more money. There's also an abundance of tasks you need to complete including admin, social media content and scheduling, programming, finances; the list goes on! It's difficult to switch off or fully relax; there's always something on your mind that you know you need to do. Inevitably, you feel guilty for taking time off that you could spend on the business.

As a result, it makes socialising even harder because it's more challenging to be 'fully present'. Unless you are a business owner it's hard to understand the pressures or the sheer obsession you have with scaling the business.

I hated the isolation (remember I stayed in a toxic relationship to avoid it before!) I needed to be around people who understood the pains and triumphs of owning a business so I joined a networking group with other personal trainers.

I invested all my time, energy and passion into the business building it from the ground up. The key word here is 'all' as I didn't have a life outside of the business. It gave my mind a positive focus; I loved the personal training aspect of helping people, but I detested the business side as it was boring, never-ending, and repetitive.

I occasionally had thoughts about changing my career to something less consuming, but I kept telling myself:

> *'No, you make decent money and you have spent years building all of this, you can't just leave it, you don't want to be a failure!'*

Leaving a career that you built yourself and invested time, money and energy into is extremely difficult and out of the question for many people. I started to go through the motions; although it was hard, I felt stuck, and I was used to it (do you recognise the pattern here?)

Body obsession

Would you listen to your dentist telling you to brush your teeth if they had bad teeth? I wouldn't; this became my thought process for personal training (another stick to beat myself with!)

I felt I had to remain lean and in shape all year round for 'the job'. However, I got obsessed with being lean and having washboard abs, so much so I would barely eat.

I was constantly exercising to burn calories believing that I needed to get leaner (which I didn't.) This obsession led to me doing something you would not expect from the stories I've already shared. As well as being a personal trainer overnight I suddenly became a policeman, a fireman, a builder, and a butler (a naked butler that is.) Did I do some fast-track training? Nope, I became a stripper. Do you remember the me at the start of this book who didn't like who they were, how they looked, and had no confidence with women? Well, it turns out I really had reinvented myself!

One of my friends from the gym asked me to do hen parties and events with him; I agreed. The money was good. I felt confident. My friend showed me a 'good 10-minute chair routine' that I could make my own (accompanied by tracks by R&B singer Ginuwine and Italian DJ Benni Bennasi.)

I was ready and took on the stage name of Magic Matt. Over the next nine months I attended many hen parties which were fuelled by alcohol, screaming women and surprised (and occasionally terrified) brides.

There are so many stories I could share, but trust me, they aren't for this book!

Who knows the dizzying heights I could have reached with that career! I stopped because I valued my weekends and I hated the pressure I was putting myself under to stay lean all year round!

I noticed that as I became skinnier my face became gaunt again; I was no longer filled out the way I once was. It frustrated me. I needed to eat more and bulk up. From someone who has had abs I can tell you they are overrated for the work and dedication you must invest to get them! Unless you are on performance enhancing drugs it's difficult to maintain a six pack, and it's even harder to make progress with your fitness because you have little to no fuel in your tank.

No pain, no gain

The following story is a combined version of events to protect identity.

I worked in a commercial gym alongside three personal trainers, including the gym manager.

The gym was constantly busy which meant you had to adapt and be creative with your sessions, especially around the peak times.

The gym manager, Pete (not his real name), had a tall stocky frame and although he might be considered intimidating because of his size, he was always smiling and friendly with others. However, I felt wary of Pete. I sensed that something wasn't quite right from the moment that I started working there.

As well as managing the gym he would also provide personal training sessions. He claimed to have lots of experience and would often remind us he was the manager for a reason. However, in my opinion his practices didn't reflect this.

It didn't seem like he cared about his clients as he was always glued to his phone each session. He simply walked around the gym and told them what to do. There was minimal coaching feedback and next to no conversations. Most of the session was filled with silence, clanging weights and phone taps. The type of routines he put his clients through are not ones I would advocate.

During my sessions I would ensure that my clients were safe and had correct 'form' so that they could avoid injury and make consistent progress. What I saw from Pete seemed to be the complete opposite. There was an imbalance in what they did, horrendous form and a high-volume of big movements including deadlifts and squats. What annoyed me the most was that I knew Pete knew how to do all these exercises correctly, but he just didn't bother teaching his clients.

Under his 'no pain, no gain' regime we would often see people walk out limping or holding their back. It was hard to stomach. If a client complained about being in pain Pete would reply:

"Goooooood, shows you're working."

Sometimes Pete didn't even give his clients a full hour. He'd often do a Houdini (disappearing act) and waste time, but because he pushed his clients to the point of exhaustion, they didn't complain or ask for more. Weirdly enough some of them got great results so maybe the intense silent treatment is a recipe for success.

It was difficult to witness his practices. He was not a good role model for the gym.

In manager mode he attempted to impose his authority with the personal trainers telling us what to do and how to do it despite us all being self-employed. Some trainers buckled and did extra for him whilst others were assertive enough to say no as it wasn't in their agreements.

He would often remind us of how expendable we were.

> *"You are lucky to be here. I could easily get a personal trainer to replace you with the click of my fingers."*

Pete's attitude towards us was very unpredictable. He could be angry, undermining us, ordering us about or acting extremely friendly with us. It was like walking on eggshells around him as you never knew how he was going to be on any given day.

The worst part, he was a bully towards staff and members, and most weren't aware. He would often sit in the office and call certain members fat, ugly or make fun of their circumstances. He would even use the CCTV screen to follow members to mock them. Members and clients are the lifeblood of the gym which secured his job, but he simply didn't care or value them.

It wasn't professional and he reminded me of my school bullies, and I hated him for it.

It wasn't a nice environment for me, the other personal trainers, or our clients, many of whom felt uncomfortable around Pete. He kept everybody on their toes.

All of the personal trainers (minus Pete) had a chat about

our concerns as we felt stuck. We wanted to leave but had no other options to rent elsewhere. We knew that certain members disliked him. They could see through the false smiles and they even overheard conversations about other members. We knew we could use this as ammo for what we were about to do.

The personal trainers gathered 30 complaints and concerns that people had about Pete. Many had evidence of their accusations proving misconduct.

An email was compiled, and we pulled the trigger by sending it to the head office.

We received a response an hour later.

> *"Thank you for sharing your concerns. As this is a serious matter, we will investigate this immediately and take the appropriate action"*

A week later Pete was fired. There were no warnings or disciplinaries for him as the evidence against his misconduct was the worst HR had ever seen. He needed to be removed immediately.

Without a word to us he left the gym embarrassed and sheepish. I don't think he ever expected us to stand up to him in any way, but bullies never do.

A new gym manager was appointed which we all felt optimistic about.

The gym started off great with the new manager; there were lots of smiles, handshakes and planned renovations (backed up by the assurance that nothing would negatively impact our training sessions.)

Things were good and the gym became more professional. It was calm. We had a good run of training our clients, helping people and making money. In the back of my mind I still had thoughts about doing something else other than being a PT, but I ignored them as the gym takeover seemed positive.

After a few months the manager started to make small changes such as different uniforms and professional policies we had to adhere to. This wasn't an issue for us, but things quickly changed.

They brought in an additional personal trainer and limited the times when I was allowed to train clients. This would negatively affect my business. I protested because it was a direct conflict. I instantly lost £700 income per month and, just like that, my trust in the manager was severed.

I didn't feel valued and I wanted out of there. The thought in the back of my mind to quit got louder and louder (no matter how much I tried to silence it.)

Stuffing my emotions

This lack of control over my business affected my mind

and brought uncomfortable feelings to the surface. Negative self-talk crept back in. To stuff the feelings down I turned to food. One day when I was feeling low, I decided to eat lots of sugary food (which I hadn't had for years.) As the food touched my lips and entered my mouth my tastebuds came alive. I had an electric feeling that instantly lifted my mood. I tried to chase that feeling every time after, but it was never caught again. I kept trying anyway.

I'd fill my basket with empire biscuits, scones, chocolate, and bread to stuff my face until I couldn't eat anymore. I felt bloated, exhausted and like a hypocrite. I felt powerless; bingeing was my attempt at regaining control, but it went on for several months. I didn't gain weight because I was doing so many workouts, but I started to lack the energy and motivation I needed to deliver high value personal training. I'm embarrassed to say that sometimes I'd reschedule my clients so that I could eat and lounge about more. I had become an emotional eater.

The question had never really left my mind.

'Should I just quit being a PT?'

It was eating me up inside, but I decided to shake up my life in a different way (part of me still didn't want the bullies of my teenage years to think I'd failed.) I decided to move back to Glasgow and do all I could to reignite my passion for personal training.

I expected to be happy. I expected to make more money and be more successful. I thought my whole life would change because I'd changed my surroundings. It did change everything, but not in the way I'd anticipated!

The return to Glasgow

I researched gyms in Glasgow and came across a large franchise that invited me for an interview. I presented well and they explained that I had to do 15 hours of classes and cleaning for them per week to be able to personal train out of the gym for free. It seemed like a good deal as I was going to be new to the area and I needed to build up the business. They liked me and I liked them; plans were set in motion.

I was excited and ready to take on a whole new chapter in the big city. I found a nice flat near Kelvingrove park that was close to the gym (and without underwear thieves or mice!) Being back in Glasgow filled me with joy; it was an escape from Inverness. People were friendlier and there were lots of opportunities. Whilst I didn't have any friends there initially, I knew I could stay connected online with my friends back home.

My marketing was pretty good by this stage so I had new clients ready to start as soon as I got there. I was going to become successful. It was time to reignite my career!

On my first day at the gym, I was very excited. The new environment provided the variety I needed. The gym had state of the art equipment, lots of open space and a buzzing atmosphere that reminded me of the gym that had originally helped me change my life. This gym had more than 5,000 members; I could see myself being very successful there. The other personal trainers seemed friendly enough. They introduced themselves and told me what they loved about the gym; this perked me up even more.

The managers explained what I would be doing on each shift; my day consisted of showing new members around the gym, cleaning and teaching a variety of classes. My shifts were Mondays 12-4pm, Fridays 5-10pm and Sundays 6-12pm which severely limited any potential social life, but I was there to work so at the time I didn't care. I thought I would be off the shifts soon enough and able to pay rent instead.

I was thrown into the deep end and told to teach a class without any knowledge of its structure or intensity. I had to make the whole thing up. Thankfully my experience allowed me to create and lead a session that members would rave about because I gave a range of modifications to suit individual abilities. I was relieved to know I had done a good job and realised that in this gym it would be a case of 'just get on with it' with very little support.

The effort I put into my classes was soon noticed by members which led to me gaining more clients for one-to-one and group sessions. It wasn't long before my schedule of clients filled up and within two months I was fully booked.

In comparison to Inverness, it was easy to secure clients in Glasgow. It has a bigger population, fitness culture is trendy, and wellbeing services are valued. This meant I could put my prices up, earn more and feel successful. My bank balance looked healthy. But the funny thing about the fitness industry is that it's full of people with big egos and toxic personalities which is ironic considering these people are supposed to promote health and wellbeing! When I got busier and earned more, I started to notice some PTs stopped talking to me, some were outright rude despite me being friendly. I didn't care; I kept telling myself I was just there to work and I didn't need to make friends with them.

To help me train more clients and make money I approached the gym manager and asked if I could pay rent instead of running their classes and cleaning for 15 hours. This would free up my time and enable me to control my business in a way that I saw fit (and I'd have my weekends back!) Doing the shifts felt like I was employed; I detested it because I wasn't fully in control!

I was told no. That wonderful thing called hindsight tells me now that I probably should have resigned there and then and gone elsewhere, but that old familiar routine kept me there once again. I was well known and liked by my clients so I waited it out.

Swipe right

As I mentioned earlier, moving to Glasgow left me quite isolated even though I was surrounded by people every day. I didn't have friends to spend quality time with and I had very little time on the weekends. I often turned to food and dating apps to fill the void.

In the first two months I met a girl, Kate (not her real name.) She was a gym member and came to my classes. We also matched on Tinder. I didn't have any other friends in Glasgow at the time and Kate was great company. We shared similar interests and she had a nice personality. It was the typical 'friend with benefits' situation. I didn't see much potential for a relationship with her; I was happy being single and focussing on my business.

But this friendship accidentally took on a new level.

Kate was a bit tipsy one of the times I met her and she asked where our friendship was going:

> *"I really like you Matt, and I want us to be more than friends. If you don't, that's cool, but I think we should go to the next level. I just need to know. You have milliseconds to decide."*

I was taken by surprise by the ultimatum. I felt pressured and realised that I may lose a friend if I didn't say yes so I committed to being with her. I was suddenly in a relationship; one that I didn't particularly want!

Kate would have been a great girlfriend for anyone; she was kind, caring and compassionate, but I simply wasn't ready for a relationship, and it showed. She invested a lot into me, and I didn't do the same as I was, you guessed it, focused on my business. I stayed in the relationship even though I knew it wasn't the right thing to do. I didn't love Kate the way she wanted me to. I saw her as more of a friend.

The isolation and my rollercoaster career (not to mention the 'surprise' relationship) started to take a toll on my mental health.

Kate was dealing with several personal issues which made our relationship very intense and removed most of the joy for me. I felt lonely but I held onto it because I wanted some sort of personal connection. It was selfish, and unhealthy for both of us.

When I connected with friends in Inverness I'd pretend everything was fine, but the truth was I was struggling.

I felt completely alone so I would eat out in cafés and restaurants most days just to be around others. However, this just ate into my profits and savings.

The need for connection led me to spend more time endlessly scrolling social media, checking for notifications, and speaking to anyone and everyone to try to fill the emptiness.

The time I spent on my phone increased as each day passed to the point that I'd barely be present.

The highlight reels that aren't real

Social media became a double-edged sword; I would get a hit of dopamine from everything good it had to offer (including funny videos, entertaining posts, and a variety of content designed to keep you on the platform), but I was also exposed to things that felt harmful for my mind.

It's just people showing the best parts of their lives through their stunning filtered photos, exaggerated achievements and hyped-up lifestyles they want us to think they actually live. When you are feeling low you don't take this into consideration, you simply see everyone else as happy and successful, which can lead to feelings of inadequacy.

Because I owned a business, I would constantly work from my phone and answer every message immediately. I'd write lots of social media posts and do lots of study to help me be more successful. I was constantly switched on.

My life became just personal training. I never switched off. When my mind wasn't thinking about work it was focused on how I wasn't successful enough. My routine included: getting up, scrolling or posting on social media, going to work, more social media, working out, social media, and sleeping. It wasn't healthy.

By giving myself little time to relax and living in the digital world of social media I started to feel an overwhelming sense of sadness. This started to lead me back to the dark hole of depression; the light started to fizzle out as each day passed.

I started to self-sabotage. I didn't feel I was worth looking after. My binge eating increased, making me feel even more like a hypocrite. I started to smoke a lot of weed to try to numb my feelings and get me through each night. The weed negatively impacted the quality of my sleep. When I woke up I was exhausted, mentally battered, and had a to-do list as long as my arm.

The combination of poor sleep, binge eating and weed became more problematic and pushed me further into the pit of depression. Exercise was my only saviour; I could go into battle with my mind by lifting weights and doing cardio. I sweated it out. It worked, for a while, until it didn't...

Pain and purpose

During a client training session, I felt a slight twinge on the side of my neck; we'd been using the boxing pads but I didn't think too much of it as I occasionally experienced niggles in my neck. I carried on like normal, but my neck became more painful and by the end of the day I couldn't freely turn my head. I decided to rest for a few days and see if it sorted itself out. It didn't.

My left shoulder also began to hurt. I could no longer do push-ups, bench press or shoulder press without pain. Over the next couple of days I started to lose all power in it. Within 10 days it had no functioning strength.

If I raised my arm out to the side you could push it straight down with your pinkie finger; there was no strength to resist. I realised my upper body was compromised. I couldn't work out, but I could do lower body exercises to keep me going. This worked short term, but within a month my hip did the same thing followed by my ankle. Less than six weeks after that initial niggle in my neck, the whole left side of my body had little to no strength. Daily tasks became a real struggle.

Even though I'd worry that I wasn't good enough or successful enough, the thought of losing my business was truly terrifying!

I carried on delivering the sessions in the gym which caused me immense pain, delayed my recovery, and crippled my mind. I could no longer fall back on the squats, pushups, running, boxing, or any sport, to support my mind. I was timid, fragile, and weak. I resorted to teaching verbally or teaching through videos because I couldn't demonstrate.

I made an appointment with a GP and sadly I was told:

> *"It's all in your head, Matt."*

They gave me no practical advice or support and didn't even test me properly. There are GPs out there who care deeply about their patients, so if you have a bad experience like I did, make another appointment with a different GP. Without any help it wasn't long before my body started to lose muscle bulk and gain fat from inactivity; now there was nothing to counteract my binge eating.

I felt unattractive and worthless, as though my purpose had been taken from me. My character changed; I regressed to the boy with no confidence who'd been bullied. The dark thoughts of the past returned and I was questioning my existence. Whilst Kate and I were still technically in a relationship, she was pretty involved in her own personal issues so not available to help me navigate mine.

Like a pack of hyenas, the other personal trainers noticed this weakness in me and abused it with bullying behaviours, which included vandalising my property. This pushed me further into depression and I didn't trust anyone in or out of the gym. I felt I needed to deal with everything on my own.

Life got worse as I increased my binge-eating, weed smoking and social media consumption without any form of meaningful connection. This created a vicious cycle that would further impact my health; I picked up frequent illnesses that would feed my depressive state.

I was living on autopilot.

I wasn't present, looking back to that time I cannot remember much. In the times I was aware of my thoughts I felt suicidal and regularly contemplated taking my life. The old questions echoed in my mind:

> *"What is the point? You will always be this skinny unattractive man that won't achieve anything so why try? You should just kill yourself and be done with it.*
>
> *You will never be valued by society for just being you. Just kill yourself. You won't be missed."*

These thoughts pushed me closer to the edge; suicide became a frequent shadow in most of my days. I'd fantasise about not having to endure the pain anymore. Everyday felt like a battle to not harm myself. I was just surviving in a lifestyle I hated, in a career I no longer wanted, and I was isolated from the world. I wanted it to end.

One night I took myself to the solace of the bathroom, which was brightly lit and absent of all noise. I stared at the white door whilst in my head I was planning how to take my life in a way that was simple and fool-proof. I didn't want to fail again. Hours flew by. I was in a darkness like no other, but before I could harm myself I heard a voice in my head:

> *"I'm not going to let you take your own life. You have a higher purpose, until you achieve it you'll not*

be able to take your life."

Whether it was divine intervention or my own self-talk, the voice saved my life that night. I returned to my auto-pilot lifestyle until a holiday with friends inspired me to set up a new future.

Chapter 3

The recovery

"I go to nature to be soothed and healed, and to have my senses put in order."

John Burroughs

I was in regular contact with my friends online and I was always making jokes and pretending to be happy in the chat, so they never knew that I needed help. I was too proud to admit how I felt to anyone as I wanted to keep wearing the disguise of being successful and proving to the people of the past what I could achieve in my life.

Out of the blue, one of my friends suggested we should go on holiday together. I desperately needed an escape so it was an instant "yes!" from me. Four of us wanted to go so to meet our strict criteria (hot, cheap, a place to party), we booked accommodation on the island of Kavos.

I finally had something to look forward to.

To prepare for the holiday I stopped binge eating so I would feel comfortable enough to swim in the pool; I began to feel healthier and look less bloated. I requested time off from the gym, which meant I would be covering someone's shifts on my return. It didn't bother me too much because I had a holiday to look forward to. I was still going out with my 'accidental' girlfriend Kate. She told me to text her every day of the holiday. I was too much of a coward to end it. I didn't want to be alone, and I didn't want to deal with Kate's reaction.

Seeing my friends for the first time since I moved to Glasgow was exciting. I hadn't realised just how much I missed them until we were reunited. It felt amazing to have real in-person friends again! As we checked in for our flights to Kavos we laughed, made jokes and caught up as thought we'd never been apart.

We boarded the plane, took our seats and listened to the safety instructions. The engines roared as the plane accelerated to extreme speeds pushing us back into our seats, and then we felt 'the lift'. We were airborne. I had escaped the gym and the life I'd created in Glasgow. I was with people who cared about me.

We had a few drinks on the plane and made jokes, setting the tone for the rest of the holiday. On arrival at the airport we were taken by bus to our hotel. We checked in and rushed off to our rooms; it was complete luxury! We had four separate ensuite bedrooms and plenty of space for our belongings. It was at least four-star quality; we couldn't believe what we got for our money.

Just kidding.

We had four beds crammed into one room, and the use of a dirty bathroom. The plumbing didn't work well so the showers stank and tasted of copper. We had to put our used toilet paper in a bin. It was a complete dump, but we didn't care. It was cheap and we were on holiday!

We got settled in then went to the local shop to pick up alcohol; mixed fruit cider was the drink of choice. It was soon time to go on our first night out in Kavos.

We went to a few quieter bars before heading to the strip where there were bars and clubs everywhere; some of them charged 10 euros entrance fee, but then drinks were free for the rest of the night. However, some of those drinks were watered down or full of ice which had the potential to make you ill as it was not made from drinking water. We came across a large, bearded man who sold us on his bar by saying his drinks were 'high quality' and his bar had a good atmosphere. We joined him and enjoyed a few drinks together. I limited my alcohol intake so I could keep my senses and stay in control, but my friends went full throttle.

We moved onto the clubs where there was pumping dance music, friendly people and plenty of dancing. We noticed that Kavos was filled with people who had just turned 18-years-old. We looked at each other and felt old as we were all in our mid to late twenties! It was a fleeting realisation, but not one that would weigh us down as we were there to have fun and hang out together. Even in our old age we managed to see out the full night.

We would nurse our hangovers by the pool until mid-afternoon most days and travel around the island to see the sights before repeating the party adventure at night. I felt alive. For the first time in a long time, I remembered what it was actually like to feel happy and free again. I didn't feel isolated because I was with my friends. I was pain-free because there was no rigorous exercise. I didn't feel stressed because I wasn't focusing on my business. It was bliss.

One day we hired a speed boat to travel around the island. Equipped with our mixed fruit cider we were ready to take on this new adventure. We spent hours chilling out, chatting and exploring under the sun. It was amazing.

The sea air was making us hungry so when one of my friends spotted a hotel in the distance, we decided to head to it. There was nowhere obvious to dock our boat so we anchored down in the sea, sealed our phones and wallets in plastic bags and jumped in the water! Keeping one hand above the water (just in case we wrecked our phones) we swam awkwardly to the shore. We took a seat (still soaking wet) and ordered delicious burgers.

The sea air, sense of adventure, feeling comfortable with

my friends and having the space to think heightened my awareness about my situation back home. I announced to my friends:

> *"I have realised that I am depressed and hate what I am doing as a job; this holiday has reminded me what it was like to feel happy again so thank you. There is a lot I need to change and I am going to make a promise that one year from now I will leave personal training and be on a different career path. I don't know what that is yet but I am telling you I will make it happen."*

Redefining me

After our holiday I reflected on what I needed to change in my life to improve my mental state and become happier. I decided to:

1. Spend less time on my phone.

I deleted my social media apps and explored ways I could dramatically reduce my screen time. This included using the app Screentime to monitor and limit my online activity. I also set boundaries and expectations of when and where to use my phone (not before I showered or had breakfast), and I moved any apps that I regularly found distracting into separate folders. This helped free up my time and reduced my exposure to negativity.

2. Walk regularly.

I wasn't exercising much on the holiday and I could no longer do heavy weightlifting or boxing, but we'd walked a lot in Kavos so I started walking around local green spaces. The daily walks cleared my mind and helped my body to heal.

3. Connect with at least one 'real life' person every day.

Even if I only chatted to a shopkeeper for five minutes I felt less alone. I knew I had to do this more.

4. Break up with my 'accidental' girlfriend.

I knew my relationship with Kate was unhealthy. I plucked up the courage and broke up with her.

These four actions helped put me back in control of my life which calmed my mind and made me feel happier.

I started to research other career options and I considered sales, marketing and project management, but none of these felt like they had the 'wow factor for me'. I asked myself what I enjoyed and the answer was 'walking in nature' so I enrolled on a forestry course in Inverness.

I handed in my notice at the gym in Glasgow. It was a relief to know I was escaping!

Monsters and angels

During my recovery period, I went home to Inverness for a weekend, and, since I was newly single, I signed up to a dating app (I would be returning to live there soon anyway.) After a few matches and online chats, I met Lauren (not her real name.) Like me Lauren had ambition and goals which I found attractive. We instantly hit it off and she came to visit me several times during my final months in Glasgow. In the city we enjoyed lots of walking, nights out, cinema trips and dinner dates. It felt amazing to have someone I could get on with. I thought Lauren was special and could be 'the one'.

She suggested that we go on holiday together and knowing how much the last one with my friends helped me I said yes. We jetted off to a Greek island with the promise of plenty of sunshine, drinks and relaxing vibes.

I know that many people find the airport experience stressful; Lauren is one of them. She found it difficult to keep her cool, but we managed to get through it and arrive on the island relatively unscathed.

We travelled, ate, drank, and had lots of fun, but (and there's always a but), there was one very odd point when Lauren had a bit too much to drink. After dinner as we were heading back to the hotel room she decided to play hide and seek in the corridors. I thought her behaviour was odd. Usually people fall over, get a bit argumentative or slur their words; hide and seek was a new one on me. Lauren kept giggling and running away. It irritated the hell out of me. What was this childlike stuff? Eventually I got Lauren back to the room and got her settled in bed, but in the back of my mind there was a little red flag.

> *'Please go away red flag. I feel connected. Lauren simply had too much to drink, that's all. It's nothing. I don't need to listen to your negativity.'*

I didn't want to see the flag so I edited it out.

The remainder of our holiday was positive. We returned to the UK feeling rested and I was all set to make the move back to Inverness. I spent my final few weeks in Glasgow organising belongings and saying goodbye to my clients. I was ready for the next chapter.

The move

On the day that my dad drove to collect me (and all my stuff) from Glasgow, Lauren was going on another holiday. She phoned to tell me how excited she was to travel and that she was in the VIP lounge at the airport where she was going to have a few drinks. I didn't think this was the best idea as I knew she had also taken Valium.

My dad and I set off on the three-and-a-half-hour drive from Glasgow to Inverness. We were catching up on each other's news when Lauren phoned again. Why was she calling me? She was due to board her flight.

When I answered I could tell she was panicking. She wasn't making much sense. She told me that she wasn't getting on the flight. She said she had been chatting with a guy and sharing a few drinks in the VIP lounge and that when she went to the bathroom he tried to sexually assault her. WTF. Lauren said that security wasn't letting her get on the flight because of this. I tried to calm her down. The line went dead.

Most people would be panicking if something like this happened to their partner, but I felt calm and collected. Part of me didn't believe what she'd said; the way Lauren described it sounded familiar. My Dad had heard the conversation and he agreed that she sounded 'off'. We both doubted Lauren's story.

My mind was searching for why the story was familiar; there was one series on a popular streaming platform which involved a bathroom rape scene which was very similar to Lauren's story.

> *'Would she make that up? Surely not. Was Lauren really capable of taking what she saw on TV and transforming it into her reality when she'd had a few drinks?'*

I didn't want that to be true. I decided that I must take her word for what happened and support her. She was my girlfriend and maybe 'the one'; I didn't want to see red flags.

Hours went by with no further contact from Lauren. By the time I arrived back in Inverness I was concerned and unsure what to do; I contacted her mum who also shared my concerns (she hadn't heard from her either.) Lauren finally called back and said she had made it to her holiday destination and she was okay. She was also very annoyed that I called her mum. It was strange; another red flag sprung up in my mind.

'Go away red flag; she has a great personality.'

While Lauren was on holiday I settled back into Inverness, spent time with friends, and explored ways to earn money part-time whilst I studied forestry.

A new idea

Although personal training had been the career I wanted to escape from, it provided good money. I decided to offer it part time at a local fitness studio which was refreshing as I could work in my own time without doing other gym shifts. As well as providing one-to-one training I looked at what else I could do to support more people to create a positive impact in a short space of time.

An idea came to me.

My mum would describe herself as a 'larger lady' and I'd already helped her lose weight and get fitter. I realised there were hardly any classes suitable for plus size women. Most classes were filled with gym bunnies so women who identified with being 'larger' often worried about keeping up.

I decided to launch a six-week women's only plus size bootcamp (an hour-long class twice a week) specifically tailored to women who were a size 16+ or had a body mass index of 30+. I wanted them to feel confident, have fun and actually enjoy exercise by starting at their level and building up.

It was fully booked within seven days.

For the first session 10 women showed up. They hadn't exercised in a long time and were naturally nervous about the session. To put their minds at ease, I introduced myself, explained the structure of the sessions and what we would be doing together. We chatted a bit, warmed up and began a circuit style session. Although I had the group working fairly hard I could see the women smiling and realising that they could do it! An hour flew by and at the end the women told me they felt happier and were excited to do the next one. This was the type of support I loved to provide.

The results showed the bootcamp was a success; each woman lost weight (some dropped a dress size.) There were dramatic improvements in fitness and the whole group felt healthier and more confident. I wanted the women in the group to feel empowered by exercise; mission accomplished.

Little did I know at that point that one of the bootcampers, Phyllis, would play a significant role in what would become known as Clarity Walk. Phyllis tended to avoid exercise, her posture was poor (her head dipped down to her chest), and she lacked co-ordination. She'd experienced a lot of hard times in her life.

Phyllis decided to become a private client in addition to attending the bootcamp. She was ready to invest in herself and her health. She worked hard and did everything I told her to achieve her goals and make significant progress. At 70-years-old she became the fittest she'd ever been. She could complete several full pushups, complex plank variations and challenging leg workouts. The training we did together wasn't particularly complicated but we created consistency that built her confidence. While it might sound like I taught Phyllis lots, believe me when I say that she is an incredible woman and without her I don't think I'd be where I am today (more on this shortly!) She is an angel.

I re-ran the fitness programme for larger ladies with some new and existing members who wanted to continue their fitness journey. The bootcamp and one-to-one work funded my first year of forestry.

The cracks started to show

I began my forestry course which gave me structure, accountability, and more friends! It felt amazing to have something new to focus on.

I'd see Lauren two or three times a week and we'd call each other every day between. We'd go on dates or hang out at each other's houses. I was enamoured by her and enjoyed her company and affection. We were inseparable and we loved each other.

However, the switch from long distance was very intense and it showed me a new side of Lauren. One that would make me start to question things.

I would often see her get highly stressed and erupt into rages. This was usually about small things which left me on edge. I didn't want to do or say anything that could potentially trigger her. I felt she enjoyed chaos. She attracted drama and spread it like wildfire using social media. Although I had allowed a harsh inner critic to inhabit my mind for way too long, I was a pretty chilled and relaxed guy when it came to going with the flow. There were now red flags everywhere.

Lauren's behaviour and negativity started to chip away at me and affected my mood. I chose to ignore these red flags. We bought tickets to see Ed Sheeran and booked a mini city break in Glasgow. On the way there we got into an argument. Determined not to let it spoil our night we went out for dinner and drinks. Once we arrived at the venue Lauren bought a few double vodkas (for herself.) I questioned her choice as I didn't think we'd enjoy the concert if we were drunk.

We found our seats and enjoyed the anticipation as the overhead lights dimmed to darkness and the stage lights began to glow. The music was loud and Ed appeared on stage to a roar of applause. He was an expert at working the crowd and instantly started to sing, play the guitar and entertain with his classic hits.

As I was absorbed in the atmosphere I turned to look at Lauren. She had finished one of her double vodkas. Her face had sunk into itself as if she was no longer there. She kept drinking and I could tell she was already drunk. It annoyed me because we were there to enjoy the concert.

I suggested she might not want to have any more. She told me to piss off. I tried my best to just enjoy the concert but I could see her character changing. I couldn't relax. I could see that the Lauren I knew was not really there. She was gone, and in her place was something or someone that I didn't like.

She started mumbling and rumbling and kicking the chair in front of her which was extremely embarrassing; it was like looking after an angry toddler. Our time, planning and money felt like it was wasted because she had more alcohol than she could handle.

I was so mortified at her behaviour that I decided we should leave so we didn't spoil the concert for the people around us.

As we approached an escalator to exit the venue Lauren was walking in front of me. Instead of stepping down the escalator steps she just walked straight forward almost plummeting headfirst. I managed to grab and pull her back; I just might have saved her life. It was terrifying.

We got a taxi back to the hotel and I put her to bed. I packed my things. She'd ruined the night and all the red flags were telling me to get out of this relationship. However, when she sobered up she convinced me we should stay together. I hoped she would learn her lesson.

Once back home I agreed to let Lauren cut my hair as she had previous hairdressing experience. It was a lot different to my usual style, but she told me how good it looked and I wanted to please her.

However, it wasn't long before the Jekyll and Hyde scenario reared its head again. The monster version of Lauren reappeared as we were planning a night out. She started to speak abusively towards my friend. I stepped in and told her:

> *"Stop that right now or we're not going out at all. That is my friend and it's not right to speak to him like that. Even if he wasn't my friend, that is not a nice way to act."*

My friend left. Lauren and I went to bed soon after.

You won't believe what happened next.

Once in bed Lauren started telling me that I was autistic. She told me that it was okay, and that there was plenty of help available for 'people like me.' She told me that admitting I had autism was the first step; It was as if she thought I was on a 12-step programme. She told me she was there to support me through it.

I don't have autism.

Then it hit me. Lauren had been watching a show about an autistic boy for a couple of weeks. In her 'drunken psychosis', she had taken what she had seen on TV and made it her reality.

My mind was spinning.

> *"That time where she said she was sexually assaulted at the airport? Did she do the same thing there? Was I right? If my earlier hunch was right then this was incredibly dangerous behaviour which could not only harm her but also lots of other people!"*

In the morning, we talked through what had happened. Lauren was offended that I would even question the airport incident but I still believe I was right. There was no police report and no court case. If something serious had happened the airport would surely have given her support and taken action? I felt terrible for not believing Lauren, but it simply didn't stack up. I gave her an ultimatum.

I told Lauren if she wanted to be with me she could drink alcohol with her friends but not with me. I didn't want to spend time with the monster side of her personality.

She told me she'd continue to do what she wanted. Lauren clearly didn't understand, or want to understand, the seriousness of her drunken psychosis. Alcohol was not her friend.

A few months earlier I had booked a holiday to Zante with my friends. When we met up one of them asked what was up with my hair. I knew it was drastically different to my usual style; it was thicker at the sides, long on top, and not very neat.

I felt as though Lauren had manipulated me. My mind was racing, perhaps she'd felt so scared that I would leave her after her toddler incident at the Ed Sheeran concert that she'd given me an awful haircut to make me look less attractive? Who knows? Either way, I felt irritated, as if the more time I spent with her the less I knew her.

My time with my friends in Cyprus was mostly like my earlier holiday in Kavos (sunshine, clubbing and good vibes), but one thing was different.

This time I drank more than normal. We were dancing with a group of girls and I got close to one of them. We kissed. I had never cheated on anyone before in any way, but I believe this was my brain's way of giving me an easy out and showing me that my relationship with Lauren was over. I was disappointed that I'd kissed this girl and even though nothing else happened I felt ashamed.

After the holiday I tried to keep the kiss a secret; I knew the devastating effect it could have on Lauren, but over the space of a week the guilt ate me up. Honesty is a core value of mine, so I confessed.

We had many arguments but Lauren said she wanted to stay with me so we tried to make it work. I was still replaying the old pattern; I did not want to be alone.

We decided to go on a city break to Edinburgh to meet one of Lauren's colleagues. I reminded Lauren to please not drink too much beforehand. Her colleague was lovely with good chat; we shared a few drinks. It wasn't too long before Lauren's face drooped and her inner monster came out to play.

She started to ramble, repeat her words and became aggressive. Her colleague couldn't tolerate her anymore and decided to leave. It was up to me to babysit her for the rest of the night.

I can't have been a very good babysitter because she picked up one of the lime wedges on the bar and threw it at the bartender. It bounced off his chest; he laughed it off. Lauren threw a second lime wedge at him. He told her not to do it again. She repeated it a third time. He warned her that next time she'd be thrown out.

Lauren had no limits. She grabbed the remaining wedge from the bowl and launched it at him. He was now riled:

"That's it! You are out of here!"

Lauren didn't like the sound of that and screamed at him

"You what!"

I could see it was about to get messy.

She threw a punch towards the bartender's face. I blocked her and restrained her just enough to remove her from the building. She proceeded to run across a busy road into a takeaway and ordered 30 nuggets whilst threatening to headbutt people nearby.

She'd crossed the line. I knew I couldn't do this anymore. I hate violence. I hated Lauren's monster alter ego.

We returned to the hotel so she could sleep off the alcohol and sober up. Unbeknown to me, in the middle of the night she decided to write a status on social media and tag my mum:

"Matt Wallace is a cheating scumbag and a horrible person. Hope you are proud of the way you have raised your son."

That's not cool.

As soon as we got home I ended our relationship. I was upset. I cried. Perhaps the version of Lauren that I loved had only ever been in my mind. She'd appeared in my life like a beacon of light when I was recovering from a dark place. Perhaps I had confused connection and intimacy with love.

I'd invested part of my life into a relationship that had gone very wrong. The 434 red flags were there, and I had ignored them all. Surely, having learnt all these lessons, my next relationship would go better? How wrong I was.

Out of the frying pan

A few months later, I fell into another relationship; unfortunately, this particular dynamic continues to affect me (more on that later.) I regret not taking time to myself to learn from all the erratic behaviour I'd already experienced.

I hadn't been looking for a relationship but one weekend my friend and I decided to go on a night out. We started at a quiet bar with a great atmosphere that I had never been to before. I ordered drinks from the most beautiful barmaid who had an amazing accent. My friend and I enjoyed our drinks and catching up with each other. After a while we were ready to move on so I left my phone number with the door staff in the hope that the stunning barmaid would get in touch.

A day later she sent me a message and we met up. Let's call her Jess (not her real name.) Jess was fun, loved to travel and was ridiculously attractive. We had great sexual chemistry which became the anchor of our relationship.

I soon realised that Jess couldn't hold her drink either, though at least her character didn't change much. When she was drinking alcohol she slurred her words and fell down a lot. It didn't take much for her to get drunk. It was frustrating, but there was one particular incident that ended our relationship.

We'd gone to the cinema to see an action film.

Before it started she ordered a couple of pints. Knowing her low tolerance I suggested she might not want to drink at 1pm. Jess replied:

"Don't tell me what to do!"

Can you see a common theme? Alcohol, arguments, me trying to prevent a problem and that becoming a massive problem...

I bought the cinema tickets and the popcorn. Jess ordered wine. It was 2pm.

The film was exhilarating. The main character was on horseback fighting people. He killed a guy with a book and had been known to kill with a pencil.

I was having an amazing time until I noticed Jess's face. It was starting to droop. I could tell she was drunk. She announced that she was going to get another drink and as she tried to walk down the cinema stairs it was like watching someone walking down the aisle on a fast-moving train. Jess was swaying side to side.

It was only 3pm!

I watched the remainder of the film and at the end waited for the cinema to empty so I could support Jess to walk without banging into people. In those few moments I clocked a very old ex - Hayley!

Often if I saw an ex I wanted to feel like I was doing better than them, but in that moment this woman had a sober man on her arm and my girlfriend was more or less passed out. In my mind I could see my ex do a mini fist pump in celebration; she was one up.

Who gets drunk at 3pm? I was embarrassed. I had low tolerance or respect for people who drink to excess knowing they can't tolerate it. I ended the relationship. We hooked up again from time to time, but we never dated again.

Having two failed relationships over the course of one college year was a new record for me (maybe I should have celebrated getting out of them so fast and not delaying the inevitable!) I realised I needed to take time away from dating and focus on myself as I was going from one relationship to another. It wasn't healthy and I was attracting (or attracted to) the wrong people.

Whilst all of this relationship chaos had been going on I was studying hard and gaining valuable experience on my forestry course. The course wasn't as outdoors based as I hoped it would be; 75 percent of it was writing plans, essays, theory work, and the infamous death by PowerPoint.

I learnt lots of interesting things including how to identify trees and plants and how to map out forestry areas for development or felling. It was also great to learn from the other students, many of whom had more experience than me.

I invested countless hours into my studies, passed the exams, achieved an A, and was all set to take on the next year of my course.

When it was time to secure forestry placements I was losing out to more experienced students. The process made me realise that whilst I loved being outdoors, I couldn't imagine forestry as a long-term career. I went back to the drawing board.

I revisited my earlier idea around sales and project management then one of my PT clients gave me an application for a local job which would change the course of my life.

Chapter 4

Clarity Walk

"In every walk with nature, one receives far more than he seeks."

John Muir

The job application that I mentioned was for the role of a green space coordinator. It was focused on creating projects to get people more active in nature around the Highlands. I had my personality to offer (see how my confidence has grown!), PT experience, and ideas that I knew could help others because they'd helped me.

I was more than passionate about this type of activity and could see myself doing it as a long-term career. I poured my heart and soul into the application and sent it off. I waited patiently for two weeks to receive an email response. I was stunned to find that I wasn't invited to an interview; I decided to screw what they thought and do a better job on my own.

The rejection inspired a new project.

According to the Scottish Association for Mental Health (SAMH) there were 805 suicides in Scotland in 2020; 54 of those were in the Highlands. I knew that if I had struggled with mental health issues (depression, anxiety, obsessive thoughts) other people would be struggling too. I knew that I could help, and I didn't need a job interview to prove it!

I thought back to what helped me and that was getting off my phone, spending time in nature and connecting with people in-person. In a bid to help others I rolled it all into one to create the UK's first 'No Phone Nature Walk.'

The idea was simple. We'd spend one to two hours in nature disconnecting from technology and reconnecting with other people; Clarity Walk was born.

I posted on social media two weeks before the first event to gauge interest. There was an overwhelmingly supportive response. Eight people booked on the walk, (including a couple of clients from my plus size bootcamps.)

The very first one took place at Craig Phadrig woods (Inverness) on Tuesday, August 6th at 12 noon. Eight strangers from different walks of life came together for the sole purpose of getting out in nature and connecting with others.

We met in the car park where I briefly explained who I was to help people feel comfortable. I explained that the purpose of the work was about connection and not fitness and we were to walk as a group. With a round of names and making sure everyone was safe to walk we set off on our route.

The walk was beautiful. The sun was shining giving us spectacular views of the Beauly Firth and the surrounding forest. It was magical for so many reasons.

The group was naturally a little nervous but it wasn't long before people started to relax and chat. For a couple of hours we were free from the pings, buzzes, flashes, calls, emails, vibrations and whistling of tech. There was nothing to take our attention away from our surroundings or our conversations. It was bliss. By the end of the walk everyone felt calmer, relaxed, connected and more energised. They wanted another Clarity Walk.

From that very first walk I could tell this was something special that could help a lot of people; I swore there and then to invest all my time, energy, and money into making Clarity Walk something that could positively impact people's lives.

I set about seeing what I could do to make this more than just a walking group. I wanted to be a support service that people could rely on. After a few weeks of research I was advised to look at a social enterprise community interest company (CIC) model. This would help me set up a non-profit company that would benefit the community. It felt like the right decision. I filled in the paperwork and put my name down as a Director of CLARITY WALK CIC.

> *Mission: To improve mental health and wellbeing through digital detox walks and activities. I wanted to help reduce isolation, reduce depression and anxiety and build stronger, more connected communities by bringing people together in nature.*

I was determined to make each walk welcoming, friendly and non-judgemental so that people could be themselves with no pressure.

To support as many people as I could I removed any financial barriers by making Clarity Walk free for people to join; we welcomed donations to help power the projects. We even set up transport systems for car shares to help people access our walks (more on this later!)

I invested my savings into buying materials, designing a logo and advertising Clarity Walk to the Inverness community. All the main decisions were influenced by the local community as I asked for their feedback each step of the way; Clarity Walk was for them!

On social media I shared my story of how I overcame suicidal depression by spending less time on my phone and more time in nature; people related to it and wanted to back the project. I was featured in the newspapers and Clarity Walk was becoming recognised. All the skills I had learnt during my PT career proved useful, especially marketing. I wasn't an expert, but I had stronger marketing skills than the majority of other third sector businesses in the area which was a major advantage to help Clarity Walk gain momentum.

The keyboard warriors

Initially my social media posts were very popular which attracted strong support, but I was also surprised to see that there was a lot of jealousy from other organisations.

People were commenting that organisations like mine already existed and there was no need for another one. I used these comments to fuel my motivation. One local charity started commenting on my popular posts in a bid to self-promote. Who does that? It's the equivalent of going into McDonald's and advertising Burger King. It's very poor etiquette.

I ignored it at first, but the charity did it three more times so I simply replied:

> *"If you were genuinely interested in collaborating to support people you would message me directly instead of advertising yourself on my post."*

He didn't like being called out in public. He sent me a direct message:

> *"I will stop advertising what we do when you stop saying your idea is unique! I have been doing this for the last 10 years and I refuse to let someone like you get in the way of that. You shouldn't be the star of this as it shadows everyone else."*

My autoresponder kicked in:

> *"Thank you for your message. We aim to reply within 24 hours."*

This seemed to freak him out; perhaps he wasn't expecting anything quite so professional. He instantly changed his tone.

"Maybe I came across a bit harsh there. I feel by saying your idea is unique it puts everyone down and we should all be working together to help people. Perhaps we can work together."

I took my time to respond.

> *"Hi [Name], Clarity Walk was set up using my own lived experience and expertise. The idea of the Digital Detox Walk is unique as nobody else is doing it. I have trademarked the name and the phrases around it. I have zero interest in working with you as you have just admitted to advertising yourself on my posts*

out of jealousy which is highly unprofessional. I understand you do great work so focus on that and I will do the same."

Then I blocked him (one of the things I do like about social media!)

There were other people who tried to put us down saying we shouldn't be awarded any funding as you don't need money to lead a walk. They clearly failed to understand the costs of systems, marketing or anything else. These people were, in my opinion, idiots. I had no time for them. There is no point in arguing with them either as they can't have reasonable discussions. I even offered to phone some of these people to chat about their concerns, but they were only happy to judge and criticise. I blocked them too.

Covering more ground

Clarity Walk began offering one walk per week, then as it grew in popularity it quickly increased to five. I was still offering personal training on the side and I loved what I'd created. I marketed heavily to reach more people. I invested in social media ads, leaflet distribution, cards and banners to spread the word that Clarity Walk was here to help (and here to stay!)

With the momentum that Clarity Walk was creating I

thought the funding would just come in. My plan was to get more people walking, get more donations and sponsorship. I didn't really have any tactics to make that happen. I had no sales strategy. There was no marketing plan. I was taking action and learning from the mistakes along the way.

At the start services were free so donations and sponsorship were hard to come by and harder to predict. Initially our grant applications were unsuccessful because Clarity Walk was viewed as a duplicate of existing services; this frustrated me as nobody systemised walks like I did or used the concept of a digital detox. I received sponsorship and donations, but not enough to sustain the costs, growth or the work I was putting in. The excitement I had about helping people kept me motivated; passion over profit.

It took quite a few conversations with local business owners and professionals to make me even consider that the model I had adopted wasn't going to work.

Super fit and super helpful

Previously, I introduced you to the now super fit Phyllis, not only was she in the first plus-size bootcamp, she was also on our very first Clarity Walk. She has been a tower of strength and support to me. She's helped me guide Clarity Walk in the right direction. If it wasn't for Phyllis,

I don't think Clarity Walk would even exist! I'll always be thankful for her wisdom, support and friendship.

With an extensive background in mental health nursing it was a no-brainer for me to invite Phyllis to be the first appointed Director of Clarity Walk CIC (in addition to me.) Her role as a non-exec director was community engagement, listening to feedback, and advising me on how we could reach and support more people.

I knew I needed help to make Clarity Walk robust but trusting others to help was extremely difficult for me as this was my baby. I didn't want to let go of the control I had over it (remember how much answering to other gym owners and PT's wound me up!) I knew that if I somehow screwed up a walk that would be 'on me', but if I involved other people I'd have to relinquish control. Thoughts like this would go round and round in my mind for weeks, but I realised that I can't expect people to be as committed as I am; I live and breathe Clarity Walk. Who could I trust? Phyllis! As well as being a director she was my first Clarity Walk volunteer. Every day she proves that I was right to trust her!

Phyllis's walks are great. She is a natural walk leader making sure everyone feels included. She was always able to keep the group walking together and engaged. Her walks became famous for her car boot café because she would share her delicious home baking at the end.

Whilst I knew Phyllis would be a tough act to follow I needed to recruit more volunteers. We created a simple recruitment process:

1. Join a walk and see if it's for you
2. If you like it, fill in the leader application form
3. Receive and learn from the notes and training
4. Co-lead a walk with another walk leader
5. When you are confident (and we are confident in your ability) you can lead Clarity Walks

I met many people who wanted to volunteer; some became great leaders and others weren't quite the right fit at that time.

I am extremely grateful for the support of all our volunteers (past and present); they are the lifeblood of our community projects and help support the people who need us most.

Within weeks of joining, I could see that members were feeling happier, more confident and enjoying each walk. It gave them structure and purpose to their week. GPs, counsellors, and mental health charities referred patients to Clarity Walk because they recognised the immense benefits.

I met many remarkable people of all ages and from every corner of life on our walks. We created a community to be proud of. Our youngest member was five years old and our oldest member in the early days was 75. Our most senior member now is 93 years old!

More than anything I think you'll be blown away by the transformational stories our members have shared (see the resources section for those.)

I was ready to use Clarity Walk to change the world, but then the world dramatically changed!

Covid-19

Clarity Walk was gaining great pace when we started to hear rumours of a virus that originated in China. We didn't pay much attention to it but then businesses started to respond by replacing handshakes with foot taps or elbow bumps. Countries began to report viral infections and it was evident that what was soon to become known as Covid-19 was getting closer to home.

Clarity Walk continued as normal. The news headlines were dominated by Covid-19. People were becoming anxious and lockdowns started to come into force. Clarity Walk was outside, and a vital support to mental health, so I expected us to be able to continue but next came the face masks and social distancing. You know how this story goes...

I searched for loopholes in the government policies and anything that could keep us going. I knew that stopping the walks at a time like this would be devastating. People needed them more than ever!

But, we had to stop. Immediately.

I had invested everything into Clarity Walk; my time, my energy and my savings. Everything I had built was stripped away. Our sponsors cancelled. The donations stopped. There was no contracted work (such as team building days.)

We were rapidly losing money; I thought Clarity Walk was over. Whatever happened next was out of my control. I didn't know what to do.

I took time to grieve. I felt like I'd failed everyone after promising to support them. The community had always been at the heart of the decisions that I made so after a few days of feeling emotional I reached out to them to ask what support they needed.

- I started posting more on social media (oh the irony) to encourage people to get out and walk.
- When I went for a walk I'd create videos to share the beautiful sights around Inverness.
- I did livestreams on social media so the walking community could at least see a familiar face.

I offered this type of support for several months (always thinking that life would go back to normal someday soon!), but we were bleeding money.

Most businesses were in a tight spot financially and the community wasn't donating to us because we couldn't deliver the walks. I had to find new ways to create sustainability.

We tried to increase donations via online campaigns; they failed miserably. I'd exhausted almost all of the other options I could think of. There was one left and it wasn't something I wanted to do, but it was something I had to do.

Paid membership

I thought about the future. People were less likely to carry cash to give to a donation bucket; I saw us rapidly becoming a cashless society with everything done by contactless payments and debit or credit cards.

After discussing the final option with the other board members, we decided to switch from a free model to a monthly paid membership of £10. Many of our members supported it, some didn't. I couldn't see another choice.

It was heart-breaking so we also offered people who were experiencing financial difficulty, those on very low incomes, or people referred to us by GP's, counsellors or mental health charities, a free membership.

The paid membership helped us survive the first lockdown as we looked sustainable to grant providers and could secure funding. There was hope!

We finally had a lifeline. After many months we received the exciting news that the lockdown would be lifted, though various Covid-19 restrictions remained in place under a tiered system. I was overjoyed as I knew I could get back to what I do best - helping people.

Once the lockdown restrictions had eased, we were able to walk in smaller groups providing we adhered to social distancing. Clarity Walk was back!

We put the news out on social media that Clarity Walk was here to help. There was a great atmosphere amongst the community and people flocked to join us, get their steps in, enjoy the sunshine and meet new people. After months of crippling stress, I felt relieved and happy that we could regain momentum.

The onset of burnout

Apart from volunteer walk leaders and the unwavering support of Phyllis, I was responsible for all the admin, marketing, accounting, fundraising, programme development and much more. Each of which would be a full-time job for most. I have utmost respect for anyone who is self-employed; it is extremely difficult to find a work life balance! I was working tirelessly to sustain and grow Clarity Walk but I could feel myself burning out. From experience burn out would arrive in two ways; it might creep up on me gradually and I'd notice myself losing energy or motivation, or sometimes it was a rapid wipe out like being hit in the face by a tonne of bricks! Sometimes I'd lose a couple of business days, and sometimes it'd cost me weeks. I'd still get what I needed done, but I'd be reduced to about 20 percent of my capability.

One burnout was triggered because an event didn't go according to plan.

This particular day had started off pretty well; people were happy and enjoying their experience but then the weather deteriorated, participants failed to follow the clear instructions set out in email, and the person we hired as a wildlife guide didn't check out the site we were visiting. He was also a bit boring. It felt like he didn't really want to be there. In my eyes, it was a disaster. Although lots of things were out of my control, it is still my responsibility to provide an incredible experience; I phoned everyone after the event and offered them a refund.

If I can't deliver something to the standard I know it should be delivered then I'm happy to offer a refund; it doesn't sit well with me otherwise. I spent the next three weeks in major burnout feeling like a failure. I was extremely anxious and lacked motivation. I could feel myself returning to self-sabotaging methods. Once again, life felt difficult.

One event lifted my spirits though. We were fast approaching Christmas; I believe that the festive season is one of the hardest times of the year, especially for people who live alone. We wanted to provide people with company through walking and talking. Seventeen people, some wearing party hats, came to our Christmas walk by the river. There were lots of smiles, laughs and we enjoyed tea, coffee and mince pies afterwards.

This walk made me feel positive and put a little more fuel in my tank because of how it brought people together. Out of the 17 people who joined that walk, only four had someone to go to on Christmas Day. It was so rewarding to know that Clarity Walk had brought people joy and social connection to those who needed it the most. It renewed my enthusiasm and energy.

It felt like Clarity Walk would continue to gain momentum, expand and develop all of our grand plans. However, a few days later everything changed again.

Chapter 5

The pain of 2021

"Mental health problems don't define who you are. They are something you experience. You walk in the rain, and you feel the rain, but you are not the rain."

Matt Haig

As a group, we enjoyed a New Year's Eve Clarity Walk so we could move into 2021 feeling positive and connected, but those feelings were soon shattered by the government announcement.

Hands. Face. Space.

We were advised that we were going into another lockdown due to the rising cases of Covid-19 during the winter months.

Everywhere I looked, I saw extreme isolation and loneliness. It was obvious to me that the mental and physical health issues that were showing themselves now would far outlast any lockdown.

I wrote to the government pleading for Clarity Walk to be allowed to continue with social distancing; how could this be considered less safe than going to a local shop? It didn't make any sense. I was told that Clarity Walk was not an essential service and we must press pause; the rage built up inside me, along with the feelings of fear that we'd lose everything that we'd worked so hard to create.

I researched the restrictions and could see that it was possible to walk with one other person so I decided this was a good way to help people. Our capacity was limited but thanks to our community network I recruited volunteers quickly; we led up to 30 one-to-one walks per week. We made the best of a bad situation and supported as many people as we could to feel connected.

Along with this, we shared live videos to encourage people to go walking, posted lots of content, and set up a new system called Online Walk and Talks (when one person went for a walk they would video call another walker, chat and share their scenery.) It was ironic because we are a digital detox company, but technology is very useful if managed in a positive way. This service allowed us to support a range of people all the way from the bottom of the UK to the top of the Highlands. It was nice to help people connect who were otherwise completely isolated.

Whilst none of us welcomed lockdown, it demanded new levels of creative leadership, not only did we arrange the walk and talks, I also created a service for children.

Children and nature

As you know, during lockdown Clarity Walk couldn't deliver in-person adult services to groups, but a local grant provider suggested I provide walking services to children under 12 (they were exempt from the restrictions.) I was told that if I could provide evidence that parents were booking their children on, then they would fund us to work with local schools. I hadn't even considered this possibility, but I knew that I could create something meaningful for them. I was incredibly grateful for the idea.

I followed the government guidelines and pulled out all the stops to create an exciting and engaging programme that children would love. We included forest exploration, den building, scavenger hunts, arts and crafts, fire building, and plenty of forest games.

For our first session we had a group of six children aged between nine and 11-years-old. They were all buzzing to get out and do something different. We (me and the Clarity Walk volunteers) introduced ourselves, explained what would happen, and did some icebreakers so the children could get to know each other.

We did a warm-up which involved nature poses, mindfulness exercises, and some pulse raising games to get them ready for a fun walk.

We also played our famous Forest Bingo (the children were tasked with finding various forest features during our walk and enjoyed ticking them off on their bingo sheets.) I taught them about the forest in an exciting way and we ran, climbed and played games over our 90 minutes together. I'm not sure who enjoyed it the most as the session allowed me to be a big kid again. I could see huge potential in offering a service for children in this way. Everyone was happy and none of us could wait for the next one!

This was a great break from the hell going on in the rest of the business. I loved seeing the joy in children's faces.

These sessions turned out to be a big hit, popular enough to make a bid to the local grant provider; we were funded to run a six-week pilot programme for local schools. I knew that this was the start of something special.

There were lots of success stories, including one young boy who had no friends before the programme because he lacked confidence and had difficulty communicating. The teachers reported that each session built his confidence and helped him engage and play with other children. After the programme he returned to school and made two new friends. It was a massive deal to him; I was so happy to have been part of it. We loved hearing from the schools and the parents how much the programme helped their children enjoy nature, be active, and get away from screens. We were making a difference in a brand-new way.

This led to us working with more schools and building a reputation locally for education, which isn't something I would have ever predicted at the start of Clarity Walk.

I was also invited to deliver a talk about how bullying had impacted on my life and what I'd done to find hope and regain my confidence. I received this message from one of the parents:

> *"Our son has just told us all about your talk on bullying; he has really taken it in. He was so sad at what you have been through and thinks you're amazing for sharing it all. We would just like to say thank you; you are an inspiring man for stepping up and speaking out!"*

Messages like this made everything worthwhile.

The children loved every session, but I knew I needed to develop the programme further. I decided to appoint a Children's Development Officer following a chance one-to-one walk with a woman who was considering becoming a member of Clarity Walk. She had years of experience, great feedback about the work we were already doing, and was supportive of our overall mission. We transformed our work with children into a five-week programme; it consisted of team building, mindfulness, therapeutic arts and crafts, den building, navigation, hammock relaxation, and fire building. With her support we began to work with more schools and gain more credibility in the sphere of education throughout the remainder of 2021.

We started to branch out into secondary schools and led an employability workshop focusing on health and wellbeing. It received lots of positive feedback and gained favour with more public organisations.

Persistence pays off

There were also further opportunities to lead workplace team building walks to help people reconnect, feel great, and encourage them to take up walking for their wellbeing. Clarity Walk was becoming more sustainable. While many of our grant applications were unsuccessful, I was determined to keep Clarity Walk afloat. Our persistence paid off:

> *"Dear Matthew,*
>
> *Thank you for applying to the Resilience fund. We are delighted to tell you that your application has been successful. We will contact you to arrange payment."*

This was incredible news. The funding supported us to develop Clarity Walk and survive the pandemic, and within the next couple of months we secured a number of generous grants.

Having spent so much energy completing administrative tasks, I knew that it was the right time to enlist help to share the load of marketing, accounting and grant applications (not to mention arranging and leading the walks!)

Misplaced trust

I was tired from running Clarity Walk all on my own. I needed support so I allocated part of the grant to pay for a virtual assistant (VA); I followed up on a personal recommendation via a local business group.

Our requirements were simple:

- Find a more efficient booking system
- Input the walks to the booking system each week
- Manage simple accounting
- Update business finances for grants
- Complete research tasks as requested

The VA that I spoke to, Joanna (not her real name), was fun and a bit quirky. She said she could take on all the time-consuming tasks. I was so grateful to have someone to help me! This also freed up my time to focus on the Clarity Walk vision, keep supporting our members, apply for more grants, and continue to develop the business.

I felt optimistic about the VA support. Joanna had been recommended, I had met with her, and she assured me she could complete the tasks. We didn't create a contract or set out terms or conditions. Although now I see that that was blatantly unprofessional from her side and mine, I paid Joanna £8,000 upfront for six months of work for two main reasons. Firstly, I believed I was unable to pay her monthly because the grant funding I used was to secure support for six months. Secondly, I was naive. It was the first time I had outsourced any work and I always expect the best from people.

It turns out my trust was misplaced.

Initially, it felt refreshing to hand over the tasks knowing that it freed up my time for more productive and rewarding work. I was happy to allocate the tasks and let Joanna use her VA expertise to meet our needs. After a month I began to question why we still didn't have a new booking system. The financial updates were delivered to me late (part of our funding criteria is that we regularly report back); I could see multiple errors in what can only be described as Excel hell. The quality of the work was abysmal.

I phoned Joanna and explained the issues that needed to be rectified; managing her was now eating into my time. She apologised. She didn't offer any extra time to correct her errors.

The second attempt was more accurate, but the presentation was poor so I fixed it myself. Red flags were marching towards me.

Joanna's 'research' into the booking system was never ending. Eventually, someone who wasn't even tasked with the job showed me a booking system that turned out to be perfect so we transitioned to it.

Each time I gave Joanna a minor task she'd miss deadlines, interact poorly or fail to deliver what I needed. To top it off I saw her VA business social media posts raving about her high-quality services. I am a compassionate person (as you've seen, sometimes to my detriment!), but I couldn't allow this situation to continue.

When I phoned Joanna she told me she was incredibly busy, had a few issues going on with her children and her own mental health etc. I am usually willing to extend deadlines (or accept a refund) if a company or person cannot follow through on their promise, but the constant excuses and poor service were really grinding my gears. Instead of being a valuable asset to Clarity Walk Joanna was costing me time, energy and vital funding! I had paid her upfront for a service that she was not delivering. I was angry at myself for not having any contractual agreement to fall back on. I had to cut my losses (before the six months were up) and move on.

I worked tirelessly to do all the tasks Joanna had failed to do (or messed up), as well as my own workload. It was frustrating to know that I had paid out £8,000 for nothing. Even if I had paid myself it would have felt better as I was getting by on the bare minimum!

I was stressed most days, suffering from sleepless nights, anxiety, and, not surprisingly, I felt low. The emotional cost of breathing life into Clarity Walk was taking its toll.

One born every minute

Remember the story I shared about Jess, the cinema drunk girlfriend? We ended our relationship and because we had such amazing sexual chemistry we continued to hook up from time to time. While I was dealing with the VA dramas, Jess came back to haunt me.

Our final hook-up was late 2020 (before the second lockdown came into force); Jess then started to date someone else and I turned my focus to Clarity Walk.

In Spring 2021 I was relaxing at home when I received a text from Jess that rocked my world.

> *"Sorry, went for a scan and I am five and a half months pregnant. It's only one week away for legal cut off period for abortion. I need £1,400 plus flights to get it aborted. Sorry."*

My only response to this text was:

> *"WTF".*

It didn't seem like the truth. I thought someone was trying to scam me, but the text was definitely from Jess.

I needed to find out more. Jess had told me that she was using contraception at the time and I did not wear a condom. I appreciate that I should still take responsibility in this situation! Lesson learnt.

Jess told me that she had been 'on the injection' but kept up the pressure for me to pay for her to have an abortion. I was in shock. The dates matched up. She said she'd gone for a pregnancy scan with her current boyfriend but was told she'd conceived before they'd even started dating. It ended their relationship. Jess said the baby could only be mine.

I doubted that I was the father of this baby. Her approach didn't sit right with me, but that didn't stop me from feeling emotional.

I had decided at a young age that I didn't ever want to become a father because I didn't want to take the chance that any other child would experience the bullying and suffering that I did. Social media adds an extra layer of bullying and that's the only future I could imagine for this unborn baby. I didn't want to pass on my genes. Having this decision taken away from me was too much; I sat in my car with tears streaming down my face. I felt completely broken.

I felt like I had failed myself and my potential child by simply not wearing a condom. It was a small decision that could have lifetime consequences.

Jess and I exchanged several messages and I met her in person. We discussed what would happen if we missed the abortion cut off period; neither of us felt ready to parent a baby. We talked about adoption which I thought might be the kindest option because it'd give a loving couple the opportunity to be parents, and give this baby a good family. Jess told me she'd give the baby to her aunt. I thought she was joking. I continued to press for a paternity test, but Jess refused. Eventually she sent me a message that said:

> *"Got it wrong by a few weeks so not yours, good luck."*

I couldn't believe what I had just read, the baby wasn't even mine! How could Jess put me through all of that without checking the dates first? Surely that is the first thing you would do! I was left in complete shock and couldn't understand why she would play with my feelings knowing I have never wanted children. I was angry with Jess and didn't want any more emotional torment. I blocked her on social media, though that didn't block out the thoughts that I might be a father.

This whole situation added to my overwhelm of trying to run Clarity Walk during a pandemic. I had focused too much on helping others at my own expense.

The heart of darkness

Even though I knew I was helping people transform their lives, I started to get swallowed up by the emotional darkness. I was drowning in self-doubt with dark thoughts creeping in and the voices of the past calling my name. I pretended everything was okay as I wanted to be seen as a strong leader.

I started to self-sabotage and isolate myself by focusing solely on the business. My body started to shut down and working out for my own health became extremely difficult; I was in pain again most days.

Although supporting people was my passion, Covid-19 had taken me away from that purpose as everything had become about financial survival. By chasing the money for Clarity Walk I lost my purpose; I wanted to quit.

My thoughts were obsessive:

> *"I should just get a 9 to 5 job. It will be much easier.*
>
> *Does the community even value what I am doing for them?*
>
> *Will this always be a constant struggle?"*

The main thing that kept me going was knowing that people wanted and relied on what we offered. I had to continue for them.

Confusion around clarity

When you're in a 'dark place', it's easy for obsessive or negative thoughts to take over. After the second lock-down people had been a bit more reluctant to commit to a paid membership in case we were put under further restrictions; this slowed down our growth. It annoyed me that people would spend £10 on junk food but not on committing to unlimited walks and support. I debated whether people in the Highlands valued the service we were offering. I compared the people here to the people in Glasgow. Negative thinking spirals do this to a person! I got more worked up thinking about how I should just pack up and head south (to Glasgow) where people were more open and willing to pay.

Despite this loud inner dialogue, I continued to advertise to bring people in because our walk numbers were low. We had initially offered car sharing opportunities for Clarity Walk events but, although noble, it was not practical because the majority of people we attracted were non drivers who expected transport to pick them up or drop them to any location that suited them just because they were a member.

We stopped advertising free transport and instead made it 'discretionary' whilst requesting that any passengers must make a donation to the driver for fuel costs.

I was incredibly stressed but trying everything in my power to make it all work; the thought that I had created

Clarity Walk and people might not want it was horrific. The voices in my head were shouting at me to quit. I felt like a failure. Here I was again! I was miserable and this time I'd created the whole thing!

Business went from bad to worse. I endured more outsourcing disasters including long overdue apps, marketing mix-ups, and fundraising fails.

Blackmail

Whilst all of this chaos was going on I received a shocking email from Jess, the 'pregnant-not-pregnant-cinema-drunk-ex'. I've paraphrased it below.

> *"Dear Matt,*
>
> *I am very upset by your decisions. I think it's ironic that you preach all day about mental health and wellbeing yet you abandoned me at my most vulnerable when I was heavily pregnant.*
>
> *Do you know how hard it was for me? Do you know how alone I felt? I cried most nights while you went out and enjoyed your life. It was immature of you to block me and try to ignore your problems. A real man would have made sure I was okay. I didn't tell anyone how you abandoned me at the hardest time of my life. I lost all confidence, but I don't think you deserve to block it out without consequences. I will have to invest time and money to feel normal again.*

I am full of anxiety.

You are the most pathetic person I know; I will never forgive you. The only thing you can do now is help me financially; I lost so much money because of maternity leave. Also, if you want me to continue to be discreet and not tell anyone you're the father of the baby, I need compensation. I never wanted it to come to this, but you literally left me no choice. The only solution in my eyes would be a one-off payment (no monthly payments etc) then we will never talk again. I won't mention to anyone that you're the dad."

I read this email in a state that goes way beyond shock. It seemed that Jess was now trying to blackmail me. I had been fully prepared to take responsibility if I was the baby's father, but she refused the paternity test and then had told me the baby wasn't mine. I was so confused.

I wasn't afraid of what Jess would tell people. I had proof that I had offered my support. I called the police and gave a statement. It wasn't a criminal matter, but they logged the details in case it escalated at a later date.

The gist of my reply to Jess was as follows:

"You previously stated on June 4, 2021 that the baby was not mine despite my repeated requests for a paternity test. You have now made several attempts to ask for money with regard to this baby. I have logged these interactions with the police.

I am not afraid of you telling people I am (or might be) the father as I have proof that I have offered to do a paternity test. The only way to resolve this is to do a paternity test. Please note, any threats will be taken seriously and will be reported."

Jess sent the most bizarre response.

"Matt, you know fine the baby was yours! The paternity request is just an easy way out for you."

I was baffled. The paternity test could only be 'the easy way out' if the baby wasn't mine; I didn't reply.

I discovered that Jess had given birth to a boy. Here's the kicker; she gave her son to her aunt who lives in central Scotland. I could not believe it; I thought Jess was joking when she said that was an option. It bothers me that I might have a son who I know very little about. I can only hope that the baby is cared for and loved whether I am his father or not.

At the time of writing this book I have decided not to push for more information or contact the aunt; I know it could be a lengthy and costly process to obtain a court order for a paternity test. Who knows how I'll feel as time goes on!

All of this chaos made me feel like I couldn't escape the darkness.

Virtual reality

Less than three months after the first VA disaster one of our members recommended another virtual assistant. I decided to meet Natalie (not her real name), as Clarity Walk still needed support. She described what she could do and sold me by asking the question:

> *"Have you worked with a virtual assistant before? If so, was there anything you didn't like about the way they worked so we can avoid those issues?"*

I explained the long list of issues. My communication with the new VA was professional; Natalie was organised and friendly. I trusted her and we got off to a great start. It was like night and day compared to my previous experience. Natalie provided useful research, did what I asked, and presented data in an amazing way. She had a good work ethic. Natalie seemed to be a great match for Clarity Walk.

I trusted her as a friend as well as a VA. Natalie recommended we make some changes to our processes, some of which were helpful. Everything went well - until it didn't.

Natalie's communication began to slip. My booking system wasn't showing the full schedule. She was missing deadlines. I offered her a break but she said she was fine; the quality of her work slipped as my stress levels soared.

We had a significant social enterprise grant application which needed up-to-date financials. I assigned the task to Natalie four weeks before the deadline. I was juggling the school projects, business development and providing membership support. Two weeks later there was still no sign of the financial reports. I could hear the distant sound of alarm bells ringing. Natalie told me the financial reports would be ready in a few days; nothing showed up. I reminded her that we were fast approaching crunch time. When the information finally arrived, it was inaccurate and incomplete. Natalie promised to update it.

We'd less than one week until the deadline. My finances were missing. I phoned Natalie. She told me she was re-checking them all and would send them the next day.

The next morning, I received a text:

Natalie:

> *"Hi Matt, on my way to A&E, sorry."*

Compassionate Matt left the building; I was filled with rage, and I didn't care why she was going to Accident and Emergency as her actions over the month severely let us down and risked us losing thousands of pounds. I should have listened to my gut and done it all myself; my gut, as we both know by now, is rarely wrong.

When I started to look through the work I'd assigned to Natalie I realised she'd been lying to me for months.

How could this have happened?

My work ethos is simple:

- Ask if you need something
- Ask if you want a day off
- If you can't do something, tell me
- Tell me if you're struggling and I'll help

I have no tolerance for lies.

Moving on

It was a big deal for me to trust anyone else after the year I'd just had.

- People had let Clarity Walk down
- People had lied to me
- People had used my good nature against me
- People had taken Clarity Walk money without delivering on their promises

I felt sad and angry. I was working twice as hard to produce good outcomes due to my poor choices in people. It was difficult to let go of the anger. Why couldn't everyone be more like Phyllis?

There had to be more good people out there. I still needed help so I looked for someone that could support me but also share my passion for supporting people and it became clear. We already had an amazing volunteer, let's call her

Angela (not her real name) who had led walks and undertaken many of the admin tasks. Angela understood Clarity Walk's vision and I was confident that she would work hard and change Clarity for the better. I wrote a contract (told you I'd learnt from that earlier mistake!) and offered it to Angela. Thankfully, she accepted and we made great progress towards improving systems and processes. Finally, I found someone I could trust and rely on. This support relieved some of the pressure I was facing by giving me more time for myself and the business.

As this was going on, I asked the grant provider for an extension and paid an accountant to sort out the mess. We successfully submitted an application and I delivered my pitch to the panel.

A few weeks later I received a phone call from one of the grant providers:

> *"Hi Matt, the panel were impressed by your pitch and the social impact Clarity Walk can provide; I am delighted to tell you that your application has been successful. We'll send email confirmation."*

I was filled with joy; this grant was different from the others as it would cover my living expenses and allow me to look after myself and focus on the business. The grant provider said they saw great potential in me and Clarity Walk. Things were looking up. I kept putting one foot in front of the other to keep improving.

With Angela's support we invested a lot of time and effort trialling new ideas and services finding out what works and what doesn't. Unlike personal training there was no blueprint to follow for this so we tried and failed multiple times, but that's okay. I started to accept failure as a positive; it simply shows you another way something can't be done. This allows you to course correct and find a new way.

With the stress I'd experienced during the year I reached out to my friends, family and directors to ask for help. They all took the time to listen to me. I told them about the business stresses, my anxiety, the pregnancy, and everything else. I was an open book; it felt great to unload my thoughts (and allowed me to receive support.) People can't help if they aren't aware that you need it. To know that people accepted and supported what I was going through helped unburden my mind and relieve some of the pressure.

Time to rise

At the end of 2021 I was in a far better headspace because I had good admin support in place, and I was asking for help. I was in a better position to reflect on the year. I realised I had dedicated everything I had to Clarity Walk without investing in myself. I had burnt out several times and my mental health was up and down like a yo-yo. I knew what I needed to do to help myself, but I just didn't do it. My mantra had been Clarity, Clarity,

Clarity, and that had to change or else there'd be no Clarity Walk and no clarity for me!

Two questions were key to help me turn it all around.

I went into my bedroom, turned off all sound and distractions, and sat on my bed. I meditated on two questions.

- What do I actually need to help myself feel better mentally and physically?
- What do I actually want?

I took 30 minutes to sit in thought until I started to receive the answers. Often when you do something like this you will get answers you're not ready to hear as it will require you to make difficult decisions.

Three answers revealed themselves to me. I needed to:

- Put myself before Clarity Walk. By looking after myself I knew I would be in a better position to look after others. It's much better to work at 80 per cent continuously, than 150 per cent and burn out every six to eight weeks. I had to put myself first to be able to enjoy what I was doing.
- I had to commit to seeing at least one friend each week; social connection is the most important thing for me to stay healthy.
- I had to stop drinking alcohol. It doesn't agree with my body. I wanted to live without it.

These three solutions weren't going to be easy to implement but I knew it had to happen. My mindset had to shift. As I made the changes I felt less pressured, could relax more, and I started to feel happier. Everything felt lighter. The thoughts that Clarity Walk wasn't appreciated began to fade as I learnt to appreciate myself. I felt optimistic once more and those three rules put me in a better position to help others (which is the whole point of Clarity Walk after all!)

My new goal of not drinking alcohol was challenged several times by social events but thankfully my friends were accepting of my choice. I even managed to survive a Stag Do (complete with private karaoke bar) in Prague without drinking any alcohol! The Stag Do showed me that if I could handle a room full of wasted guys and a karaoke booth whilst sober then I could handle anything.

A few weeks later my friend John (the stag) married the love of his life, Laura. The ceremony was beautiful and the reception was well organised with a live band and lots of fun activities. I was singing, dancing and having fun; sober Matt was here to stay, and it's just as well, because it wasn't long before someone asked for my support at a whole new level.

A call for help

"Hi Matt,

I know the great work that you do with Clarity Walk and someone suggested that I reach out to you to see if you could help. My son recently tried to commit suicide by jumping in front of a car. It really scared us both. I was wondering if you could walk with him one-to-one?"

I replied:

"Thanks for reaching out. I am very happy to help. Please note that I am not a psychologist or mental health professional of any kind; I am simply a man who is willing to listen."

We agreed on a date and I took the young man for a walk in a local forest. At the start of the walk he seemed quite low (as you would expect.) As we wandered through the forest I listened to him and asked open ended questions. The walk was just an opportunity for him to be himself with no judgement. During our time together he came up with solutions of his own and action steps he could take to feel better. By the end of our 90-minute walk he seemed happier, more hopeful, and was able to take on the coming days and weeks.

I asked him why he'd wanted to meet me rather than go to his GP or phone a crisis line. He told me that our time together seemed more accessible with less expectation or the label of 'mental health issues.'

This situation inspired a new idea. When I started Clarity Walk, I had primarily planned to support men but I knew that sometimes they're harder to engage. They often seek certainty and proof that something works and at the start I couldn't provide that. Instead, I focused on anyone who needed help.

The mental health statistics in the Highlands for depression, anxiety and suicide all show that men are at higher risk than women, even more so in rural areas. A lot of men meet new people and socialise in pubs, which isn't the healthiest of routines.

There were a few support groups but they didn't seem to be making their mark. Also, the ones that offered sport activities would not appeal to the men who didn't have the confidence to participate in a skill-based activity.

Wellbeing activities are traditionally dominated by women, even Clarity Walk was more than 85 percent female; that fact alone might put some men off!

I could see that men needed a service that was specifically for them.

I shared the idea on social media for a 'Men's Only Project' allowing men to walk and talk with other men. It was well received but took much longer to get engagement and sign ups.

On December 21, 2021, we had 11 men on our first Men's Only Walk. I thanked everyone for being part of such a momentous occasion as I knew they would help other men to reach out and get involved. It was heart-warming to see men from all different backgrounds connecting with each other as we walked. At the end everyone felt refreshed, connected, and motivated to take on the day. We enjoyed hot drinks before everyone departed.

I began campaigning for the men's only project and arranged events every three to four weeks as I knew it would take time to build momentum. The mission for the project was simple; build a men's community to reduce isolation and improve their mental wellbeing.

Most people were in full support of it but there were a few that were completely against what I was doing commenting that I was sexist, misogynistic and referenced the patriarchy a few times as they clearly had nothing better to do. I rarely replied to those messages and continued to focus on my mission.

I received several donations in December 2021 from people who did support the project; these helped propel us forward to be a positive force for change.

2021 was a difficult year. We had been shut down by lockdowns and mishaps. However, we still managed to accomplish a lot in the year.

- We survived two lockdowns and had 3200 attendees join our walks and activities
- Created a children's program supporting over 150 children and multiple schools

- Collected 4600 litres of rubbish from local nature spots
- Provided 10 volunteering opportunities

The year ended well and things were looking up for both myself and Clarity Walk.

Chapter 6

Walking forward

"Self-care is how you take your power back."

Lalah Delia

In the first six months of 2022, we were able to reap the rewards of our hard work. Clarity Walk has gained new members, free publicity, grants, and continues to develop its services. Everything was falling into place. I was feeling happy and proud of what I was doing as it was truly making a difference. There were some days where I would need to take the day off or work a half day due to my headspace, but I no longer punish myself for this and accept it for what it is; I know this is going to help me and Clarity Walk in the long run.

In this time, I found peace and solace hiking in the mountains. It allowed me to disconnect from Clarity Walk and truly focus on myself. I found the mountains brought a new level of discovery that challenged me mentally and physically. The hikes restored my energy and allowed me to think with a clear mind. I conquered many Munros and Corbetts, often wild camping to spend days in the hills and mountains.

I wanted to share this experience with others, so I started to work towards my mountain leader qualification. This involved improving my navigation skills, gaining group leading experience and learning how to work safely in the mountains.

To help me qualify I started a small project called Matt's Mountain Days to build a group of keen adventurers who I could lead in the mountains. This was very rewarding as I could show people the power of the hills. It would allow them to completely switch off, explore beautiful Highland locations and feel invigorated from the time spent in nature. I knew it would be a great addition for what Clarity Walk could offer and what I could offer.

In my mind I knew there was one change I needed to make for Clarity Walk now that we were on the other side of the pandemic. If you remember, we changed to a paid membership model following the first lockdown. It allowed us to survive. This wasn't something I ever wanted to do; it was something I had to do. With other services in place, I felt we could finally return to the no-fee membership.

I met with my directors and we discussed the pros and cons of switching from our paid membership model to a no-fee membership. This would once again be powered by donations, sponsorship, and our other services. There were a few reasons we made the switch, the main one being that we could support more people as they wouldn't see cost as a barrier to joining (which meant we created a larger impact in the community.)

Secondly, it would allow me to enjoy running the organisation because it would remove the expectations people placed on us and enable us to go at our own pace.

Thirdly, removing the paid membership model would allow us to expand to other locations because we could start in areas with just one walk every three weeks and slowly build up (because we weren't dependent on people joining and paying us money.) There were a lot of positives to returning to a no-fee membership. I could see no downside.

Full of excitement, we announced the switch using social media posts and live videos to explain why we were doing it and thanked everyone who supported us over the years, including our members, sponsors, grant providers, volunteers, and anyone else who helped us along the way. People were delighted that we made the change, and many members chose to turn their membership fee into a donation, which we are extremely thankful for.

Through the pandemic our identity became mixed as we tried multiple different services, including foraging, bushcraft and other themes for day events and team building days. We decided to remove all of that and just be known for walking and hiking to show the power of a Digital Detox Walk. This would keep us on brand so we are seen as experts who are passionate about our work.

With all the positive decisions we made Clarity Walk attracted lots of new business opportunities. This included educational programs with primary and high schools, wellbeing and employment programs with public organisations and a variety of private teambuilding days. This allowed us to become more financially sustainable with less reliance on grants.

As the managing director I had to make difficult decisions in 2022 but they were made with a clear mind which led to more positive outcomes for myself and Clarity Walk.

Like any other business we still face many challenges but our dedication and hard work has helped propel us in the right direction so we can achieve our potential and support those in need. However, this is just the beginning of the Clarity Walk story. Clarity Walk will be a name that is heard beyond the Highlands, and by you purchasing this book you help us to achieve that. Thank you.

I never dreamed that I would be able to confront my pain from bullying and depression and use it to change not only my life but others as well.

There are still days where I struggle and doubt myself, but I now ask for help, slow down, and invest in myself, and make sure I stay connected to others. I often remind myself of how far I have come. My story started with the boy who was relentlessly bullied and had no hope and ended with the man who has supported thousands of people by creating an enterprise from his pain. This is something I can be proud of.

This journey has been transformational with many lessons learnt. I would like to share those lessons to support you or someone you know.

Closing thoughts

Right now, I feel more fulfilled, more optimistic, and I am enjoying life again to take on new challenges, develop myself, and make the most of every day. In addition to making a tangible difference to the lives of people who were otherwise suffering in silence it's created a massive shift in my life. I have more clarity than ever, and I've learnt some valuable lessons along the way.

Here are 10 of the lessons I've taken on board (see if some of these will work well for you.)

1. The power of connection.

Friendships and meaningful connections are 'everything.' They helped me to enjoy life, have a feeling of purpose and reduce my sense of isolation. Even if you only spend quality time with one person per week you will feel the benefits. There are lots of social groups and activities out there; choose what will help you feel connected.

2. Ask for help.

There are people out there (friends, family, colleagues and professionals) who are willing to help you through dark times; you just have to summon the strength to ask for it. I worked with a therapist in my teens, and when I started writing this book I hadn't anticipated how much trawling through distressing memories might affect me. The first therapist I reached out to wasn't a good match, but I didn't let that stop me. I followed up on a recommendation from a friend and that counsellor turned out to be a great support. Don't suffer in silence.

3. Be open to what's possible.

I didn't see myself as someone who would enjoy public speaking, working with children, or being the founder of a social enterprise, but it has led to many positive opportunities that I am very thankful for. Don't stand back: take the leap and find your opportunities.

4. Acknowledge and act on your red flags.

I was tempted to make every page of this book red due to the number of red flags that I was writing about! As you'll know by now, often when I noticed a red flag I ignored it. I now acknowledge them, trust my intuition and find solutions to deal with them. Pretending everything is fine is a recipe for disaster; sometimes the solutions are not our first choice, but learning to become more assertive, have difficult conversations, and end relationships are essential parts of self-care.

5. If at first you don't succeed, try again.

Clarity Walk was not a success from the outset. I've openly shared my failures with you; there were so many mistakes I had to learn from. Success doesn't happen overnight. When you become more comfortable with what you perceive as 'failure', you'll find it easier to adapt, do something different, and succeed.

6. Prioritise your own happiness; invest time and energy in you.

Prioritising yourself allows you to be the best you can be. You will benefit from taking time out to go for a walk, prepare healthy meals, be with friends or read a book. Until you top up your own cup you can't freely give yourself to anyone or anything. You have to be selfish before you can be selfless.

7. Set personal goals.

When you set personal goals, you're actively directing your life; how much better does that feel than being constantly tossed around by whatever comes your way? I enjoy setting personal goals as they motivate and give me something to work towards. For example, set yourself a 90-day goal of what you want to achieve and the simple steps that will take you there; this might include preparing meals in bulk three times per week to help you improve nutrition with the goal of feeling healthier.

8. Define your own version of success (don't believe the highlight reels.)

If you try to match the definitions of success that you see on social media you've likely committed yourself to a life of misery. You do not have to have a career that earns megabucks. You don't have to have millions of social media followers. You do not have to be married or have children or be a certain weight or drive a certain type of car! You get to decide what makes you happy and that is the best definition of success you'll ever find!

9. You are not your past.

If you've read this far, you'll know that I was bullied and frequently told that I 'wouldn't amount to anything.' It affected me but I didn't allow it to define me for the rest of my life (though I did wallow in it for a while.) I was determined to break free from the past and prove to myself (and those pathetic bullies) that I could make something of my life and be happy. You can do it too.

10. Take full accountability for everything

By taking accountability you feel more in control to make the changes needed and achieve positive outcomes in the future. You are responsible for your decisions and your mistakes. As much as people can support you to make decisions, accountability lies with you. Take accountability of everything to fix what you can, accept what you can't and ignore what doesn't directly affect you.

What's next for Clarity Walk?

Clarity Walk will continue to grow, support, and evolve in a positive way to reduce isolation through its activities. It will:

- Expand throughout the Highlands to support people in remote and rural areas
- Offer franchise opportunities in other towns and cities outside the Highlands

Clarity Walk has a fantastic team right now and the future is exciting.

Will I manage Clarity Walk forever?

You know how I love to set goals and transform my life. Right now, I am building my own personal brand (public speaking and Matt's Mountain Days.) I am also expanding my passion for supporting people into the coaching arena.

It's difficult to say if I will be managing Clarity Walk long term, but whatever happens I will always make sure that its members, staff, and volunteers are always taken care of so that it remains a steady service for others.

No-one has to walk alone.

If you are ready to take the step to your own clarity you can:

1. Come and join us on a Clarity Walk if you are in the area.
2. Become a volunteer walk leader (or see what other roles might be available.)
3. Start your own group if you're outside the Highlands (franchise.)

Get in touch with us via www.claritywalk.co.uk.

I hope my story has shown you that even with the darkest days and darkest times you can make it out to feel happier, improve, and feel accomplished in whatever you choose to do. Things do get better; I am rooting for you.

All the best,

Matt.

Resources

There have been a range of topics in this book which may affect you or someone you know. Here is a list of useful resources:

Mental health support

- The **NHS** website offers a list of services www.nhs.uk/mental-health/
- **Mind** provides advice and support to empower anyone experiencing mental health issues www.mind.org.uk or call 0300 123 3393
- **Samaritans** provides 24/7 listening and support for anyone in emotional distress www.samaritans.org or call 116 123.
- **Sane** provides help for anyone affected by mental illness, their carers and families www.sane.org.uk or call 0300 304 7000.

Substance misuse

- **We are with you** is a service that offers support and advice for anyone experiencing alcohol or drug issues www.wearewithyou.org.uk
- **Frank** provides honest information about drugs and substances and how to get support www.talktofrank.com or call 0300 1236600.
- **Alcoholics Anonymous (AA)** supports personal recovery and continued sobriety with support groups www.alcoholics-anonymous.org.uk/ or call 0800 9177 650.

Gambling support

- **Gamcare** provides support and advice for anyone experiencing gambling issues www.gamcare.org.uk/ or call 0800 8020 133.

Mindfulness exercises

Walking

Needless to say, I am a big advocate of walking for mindfulness; it has countless benefits. It will help you lower stress, improve your mood and give you more energy. All you need is a pair of trainers/walking boots and comfortable clothing. You can often find great walks by searching 'walks near me' on google. Your walk can be done solo, with someone you know, or with a walking group. Commit to at least 20 minutes and walk anywhere in nature and pay attention to the sights, sounds and smells on your route. This will to help you switch off to feel calm and relaxed.

4, 7, 8 Breathing

When we are feeling stressed or anxious our heart rate rises and our breathing pattern changes which creates more stress. Regulating your breathing can take you into a calmer, relaxed state.

4,7,8 Breathing is a simple technique:

1) Inhale through your nose to the count of four
2) Hold your breath to the count of seven (unless you are pregnant or suffer from any respiratory issues in which case seek advice from your GP.)
3) Breath out through your mouth to a count of eight

Each time you do this breathe in through your nose and out through your mouth with gently pursed lips repeating 1-3 a total of 10 times. Adapt the breath if you find it challenging to meet the count; all you need to do is keep the ratio roughly the same.

Brain dump

Writing this book has been very therapeutic for me as getting thoughts out of my head and onto paper helps to unload the brain. You can do a concise version of this with an activity called a brain dump.

Grab a pen and paper and write down everything that is on your mind. It helps to clear the mind and make sense of what is going on. Spend 10 minutes on this exercise.

Authentic self

Being your authentic self is important for a healthy mindset. Grab a bit of paper and simply write who you really are deep down and what makes you happy.

Take 10 to 30 minutes to do this in a quiet room free from distraction; after you complete it reflect on what you have written and how it compares to how you are living right now to see positive actions you could take.

Remember that you may have to make difficult decisions to get where you want to be (but it pays off.) Write down at least three positive actions you could take to help transform you you're feeling right now.

Case study

Natasha's story

Natasha suffered from crippling anxiety which was controlling her life. It got to the point that she couldn't put her rubbish bins out for collection as she feared she'd be judged for leaving the house. She wanted to change but didn't know how; she saw one of our adverts on social media and decided to get in touch then booked a walk with us.

To help ease her nerves I met her alone to have a quick chat before introducing her to the larger group. It wasn't long until she started chatting with many of our regulars. She realised that Clarity Walk was a safe place free from judgement. It was safe for her to be herself, relax, and use nature as her therapy. Booking at least two walks per week Natasha became a regular. She was always smiling and adding good vibes to the group. Each walk reminded her what it was like to laugh and smile again.

Three months later she felt in control of her anxiety to the point she was socialising and going on nights out (not just putting the rubbish bins out!) Clarity Walk changed her life. You can listen to Natasha's powerful stories (and more!) on our website at:

- www.claritywalk.co.uk/testimonials

Enjoyed this book? You can make a big difference

Unfortunately, I don't have the financial might of a big-time publisher. I cannot take out website features, put up posters at bus stops, or appear on TV chat shows.

But I do have something that is more powerful and effective. That is the support of my readers who are keen to be loyal and supportive.

My supporters know my mission and the importance of reaching more people with this book to transform lives.

Honest reviews help increase our reach to get this book into the hands of those that need it most and steer away those looking for a different story.

If you've got something to share about this book, I would be very grateful if you could spend just a minute or two leaving a review (it can be as short as you like) on the book's Amazon page.

Spreading the word on your social media channels will also help.

Let's keep in touch

Let me know how you're doing. Email me at matt@claritywalk.co.uk and join my email list on www.claritywalk.co.uk/mywalktoclarity

Join me on my Matt Wallace social media channels

Facebook - Search Matt Wallace to find me
Matt's Mountain Days

- /mattsmountaindays

Instagram

- @matt_wallace2019

LinkedIn

- Search Matt Wallace on LinkedIn to find me and look out for the photo

Work with me

There are three ways you can work with me.

Teambuilding walks
Digital detox walks and mountain hikes to support your team to connect, refocus and improve mental wellbeing.

Public speaking
Whether it's a corporate event, private meeting, or a public seminar; I can share my powerful story and expertise to support your audience.

Coaching
1 to 1 coaching online providing direct support so you take the action needed to become mentally and physically stronger.

To find out more, visit:

- www.claritywalk.co.uk/workwithmatt

Scotland's leading dental group
clydemunrodental.com

Health and performance, naturally
niallrooney.co.uk

Your local recruitment experts
brookstreet.co.uk

Highlands based Ecological Consultants
a9consulting.co.uk

Inverness Taxis
inverness-taxis.com

Printed in Great Britain
by Amazon